WORLD OF GRAMMAR AND WRITING

1

NATIONAL GEOGRAPHIC
LEARNING

Australia · Brazil · Mexico · Singapore · United Kingdom · United States

Contents

Grammar

Writing

Subject pronouns and present simple: *to be*

Subject pronouns

Singular	Plural
I	it
you	we
he	you
she	they

Subject pronouns show who or what something does or is.
I am happy today.

We use *it* for things or animals. But if the animal is a pet, we often use *he* or *she*.
Look at the dog. It's very big.
I love my cat. He's funny.

We use *you* for the singular and the plural.
You are a good friend, David.
You are good friends, John and Sarah.

We use *they* for two or more people, animals or things.
Where are the boys? They are in the park.
Are dolphins clever? Yes, they are.
Where are the pens? They're on the table.

1 **Write the subject pronouns.**

1 Uncle John _____he_____
2 the cat _____
3 Lucy _____
4 my mother _____
5 Mum and Dad _____
6 my friend and I _____
7 the TV _____
8 the books _____

Are you happy, Dad?

Yes, I am!

Present simple: *to be*

Affirmative	Negative	Question
I am (I'm)	I am not (I'm not)	Am I?
you are (you're)	you are not (you aren't)	Are you?
he is (he's)	he is not (he isn't)	Is he?
she is (she's)	she is not (she isn't)	Is she?
it is (it's)	it is not (it isn't)	Is it?
we are (we're)	we are not (we aren't)	Are we?
you are (you're)	you are not (you aren't)	Are you?
they are (they're)	they are not (they aren't)	Are they?

Short answers

Yes, I am.	No, I'm not.
Yes, you are.	No, you aren't.
Yes, he is.	No, he isn't.
Yes, she is.	No, she isn't.
Yes, it is.	No, it isn't.
Yes, we are.	No, we aren't.
Yes, you are.	No, you aren't.
Yes, they are.	No, they aren't.

We use *to be* to talk about someone's job, nationality, relationship, or his or her name.
*He **is** a doctor.   She **is** my sister.*
*We **are** Italian.   I **am** Gianna.*

We also use *to be* to describe people and things.
*We **are** happy.*
*The sea **is** blue.*

In everyday English, we use the short form.
*Hi. I**'m** Susan.*

We use *to be* with subject pronouns (*I, you, he,* etc.) and other words.
*He **is** sad.*
*The ball **is** green and red.*

2 **Complete the sentences with the present simple of *to be*.**

1 He _____ is not _____ happy today. ✗
2 You _____ funny. ✔
3 I _____ hungry. ✗
4 The flowers in the garden _____ very pretty. ✗
5 The TV _____ in the kitchen. ✗
6 The forest _____ near our house. ✗
7 The books _____ on the chair. ✗
8 Anton and Luca _____ friends. ✔

Think about it!

In English, *you* can be singular or plural.

3 **Circle the correct answer.**

1 *I* / *We* am a good student.
2 Is *you* / *he* clever?
3 *We* / *She* are tired.
4 *He* / *I* is at school.
5 *They* / *She* are English.
6 Is *she* / *they* in the bedroom?
7 *We* / *He* aren't in the garden.
8 *She* / *I* isn't in the kitchen.

5

4 **Complete the questions with *am*, *are* or *is*. Then answer the questions.**

1 ___Are___ you at home now? ✔

___Yes, I am.___

2 _____ the clothes on the bed? ✗

_____

3 _____ the computer on the desk? ✔

_____

4 _____ I clever? ✔

_____

5 _____ breakfast ready? ✔

_____

6 _____ she outside the door? ✔

_____

7 _____ we at the right house? ✔

_____

8 _____ the cake in the basket? ✗

_____

Think about it!

Affirmative short answers do not use the short form of *to be*.

Present simple: *to be* – negative questions

Negative questions

Aren't I?
Aren't you?
Isn't he?
Isn't she?
Isn't it?
Aren't we?
Aren't you?
Aren't they?

We use negative questions when we expect the answer: 'Yes'.
Isn't it hot today?
Yes, it is. It's very hot.

5 **Complete the questions with *aren't* or *isn't*.**

1 ___Aren't___ I clever?

2 _____ she ready?

3 _____ he at work today?

4 _____ the vegetables in the basket?

5 _____ they angry about the broken window?

6 _____ the chocolate cake good?

7 _____ you tired after your walk?

8 _____ the teacher happy with your work?

Think about it!

The negative question for *I* is *Aren't I?*

6 **Rewrite the sentences and questions with subject pronouns.**

1 <u>The restaurant</u> is next to the sea.

   <u>It is next to the sea.</u>

2 <u>Nikolas</u> isn't on the bus.

   _____

3 Isn't <u>the actor</u> good?

   _____

4 <u>My family and I</u> are very happy to see you.

   _____

5 Is <u>Aunt Emilia</u> on the phone?

   _____

6 <u>Mum and Dad</u> aren't in the kitchen.

   _____

7 **Write sentences and questions with *to be*.**

1   you / be / tired / today / ?

   Are you tired today?

2   the sea / be / very warm

   _____

3   I / not be / tall

   _____

4   the books / be / on her desk

   _____

5   our friends / not be / at home at the moment

   _____

6   you / be / ready / for lunch / ?

   _____

7   my parents / be / very busy / at work

   _____

8   she / be / at the café now

   _____

8 **Complete the text with *is, isn't, are* or *aren't*.**

¹ _____Is_____ Aki happy today? Yes, he ² _____ . It ³ _____ a beautiful day. The sky ⁴ _____ cloudy; it ⁵ _____ blue. Aki ⁶ _____ at school today. He ⁷ _____ by a river, watching the ducks. The ducks ⁸ _____ hungry! His grandparents ⁹ _____ at home. They ¹⁰ _____ with Aki. Aki's parents ¹¹ _____ watching the ducks. They ¹² _____ at work!

Pairwork

Work in pairs. Take turns to ask and answer the questions below.

- Is it sunny today?
- Are you at school now?
- Is your mum at home now?
- Are your school books heavy?
- Is your best friend with you now?

- Are you hungry?
- Are you thirsty?
- Is it hot outside?
- Is it lunchtime?
- Is this activity easy?

Writing

Write. Include the points below.

- where you are now
- what the weather is like
- where the other members of your family are

Articles, regular and irregular plurals

The indefinite article

a		an	
a book	a horrible day	an ant	an island
a garden	a star	an adventure story	an orange bag
a girl	a uniform	an egg	an owl
a green apple	a yellow ball	an hour	an umbrella
a house		an interesting lesson	

We use the indefinite articles *a* and *an* with singular nouns.
a *girl*   **an** *egg*

We use *a* before a consonant (*b, c, d, f, g, h, j, k, l, m, n, p, q, r, s, t, v, w, x, y, z*) and *an* before a vowel (*a, e, i, o, u*).
an apple   **a f**ilm

Sometimes there is an adjective before the noun. When the adjective begins with a consonant, we use *a*. When it begins with a vowel, we use *an*.
a green apple   **an i**nteresting film

We use *a* or *an* to talk about one person, animal or thing in general.
(We don't use *a* or *an* to talk about someone or something specific.)
*There's **a man** outside.   **A bag** is on the table.*

Notes

Be careful! Some words begin with *h* or *u*. When the word begins with a consonant sound, we use *a*. When the word begins with a vowel sound, we use *an*.
an hour, **an u**mbrella, **an u**ncle
a hat, **a h**ospital, **a h**otel, **a u**nit, **a u**niversity, **a u**niform

What can you see?

I can see the sky, clouds, a bridge, a train and trees.

1 **Write *a* or *an*.**

1 _____an_____ island

2 _____ zoo

3 _____ clock

4 _____ octopus

5 _____ kite

6 _____ doctor

7 _____ aunt

8 _____ hotel

9 _____ hour

10 _____ elephant

2 **Write *a* or *an*.**

1 _____a_____ clever girl

2 _____ exciting film

3 _____ interesting book

4 _____ happy child

5 _____ yellow coat

6 _____ red umbrella

7 _____ awful day

8 _____ big house

9 _____ orange notebook

10 _____ useful lesson

The definite article

the

The moon is white.
The Atlantic Ocean is very big.
The green books are on the table.

We use the definite article *the*:

- to talk about specific people, things or animals (singular or plural).
  ***The* boy in *the* red T-shirt is outside.**
  ***The* blue trousers are on *the* bed.**

- to talk about something that is unique.
  *Look at **the sky**. It's so blue!*

- with the names of mountain ranges (***the** Himalayas*), oceans (***the** Pacific Ocean*) and seas (***the** Black Sea*), rivers (***the** Thames*) and deserts (***the** Sahara Desert*).

- with musical instruments.
  *He plays **the** guitar.*

We don't use *the*:

- with people's names.
  ***Paul** and **David** are best friends.*

- with the names of countries.
  (But we say: ***the** United States* (***the** US*), ***the** Netherlands*, etc.)
  ***China** is an interesting country.*

- with subjects, games or sports.
  ***History** is my favourite subject.*
  *They play **hide-and-seek**.*
  *She plays **basketball**.*

- when the noun is plural and we are talking about people, animals or things in general.
  ***Giraffes** are very tall animals.*
  *I like **films**.*

3 **Complete the sentences with *a*, *an* or *the*.**

1 There is _____a_____ book on the table. _____ book is interesting.

2 There is _____ table in my room. On _____ table, there is _____ bowl. There is _____ apple in _____ bowl.

3 Mexico City is _____ very big city. In _____ city, there are millions of people and millions of cars.

4 Look! There is _____ man in _____ street. _____ man has got _____ umbrella. _____ umbrella is red and white.

4 **Complete the sentences with _the_ or –.**

1 My cousins are on a skiing holiday in _____the_____ Alps.

2 I like _____ history.

3 She lives in _____ US.

4 My cousin plays _____ drums.

5 _____ Nile is a long river.

6 _____ sun is very hot today.

7 Tourists go to _____ Paris to visit _____ Louvre art gallery.

8 Red Square is in _____ Moscow.

Regular plurals

Singular	Plural
boy	boys
bus	buses
brush	brushes
dress	dresses
fox	foxes
leaf	leaves
party	parties
pencil	pencils
photo	photos
tomato	tomatoes
watch	watches
wife	wives

We usually make a noun plural by adding -s.

chair   →   chair**s**
table   →   table**s**

We add -es to words that end in -s, -ss, -sh, -ch and -x.

dress   →   dress**es**
fox   →   fox**es**

When a word ends in a consonant and -y, we take off the -y and add -ies.

baby   →   bab**ies**

When a word ends in a vowel and -y, we just add -s.

key   →   key**s**
birthday   →   birthday**s**

Irregular plurals

Singular	Plural
child	children
deer	deer
foot	feet
goose	geese
man	men
mouse	mice
person	people
sheep	sheep
tooth	teeth
woman	women

We usually add -s to words that end in -o. Sometimes we add -es.

piano   →   piano**s**
photo   →   photo**s**
tomato   →   tomato**es**
potato   →   potato**es**

When a word ends in -f or -fe, we usually take off the -f or -fe and add -ves. But we just add -s to the words _giraffe_ and _roof_.

wife   →   wi**ves**
half   →   hal**ves**
giraffe   →   giraffe**s**
roof   →   roof**s**

Irregular plurals do not follow any rules. You must learn them.

5 **Write the plurals.**

1 knife _____knives_____

2 piano _____

3 table _____

4 tomato _____

5 sandwich _____

6 country _____

7 box _____

8 dish _____

9 address _____

10 plane _____

6 **Write the plurals.**

1 sheep _____sheep_____

2 mouse _____

3 man _____

4 tooth _____

5 goose _____

6 person _____

7 child _____

8 foot _____

9 woman _____

10 deer _____

7 **Complete the sentences with the plural of the word in brackets.**

1 Six _____sheep_____ (sheep) are in the field.

2 Ten _____ (person) are on the bus.

3 Two _____ (man) are in the street.

4 Three _____ (boy) are playing computer games.

5 A lot of _____ (child) are in the playground.

6 He's got big _____ (foot).

7 Her _____ (tooth) are very white.

8 The _____ (pizza) are ready now.

9 There are four _____ (glass) on the table.

10 We've got two _____ (video game) for the weekend.

Think about it!

We say *one* instead of *an* when we are counting.

8 **Find and write ten plural words.**

1 p _e_ _n_ _s_

2 s __ __ __ __ __ __ __ __ __ __ __

3 t __ __ __ __ __

4 h __ __ __ __ __ __

5 f __ __ __ __ __

6 b __ __ __ __ __ __ __

7 p __ __ __ __ __ __ __

8 l __ __ __ __ __ __

9 c __ __ __ __ __ __ __ __

10 m __ __ __

B	O	F	P	S	E	P	E	N	S	T	O	R
A	B	O	C	N	S	A	G	D	O	C	X	M
Z	R	X	I	O	P	R	H	O	U	S	E	S
B	U	E	L	A	T	T	N	A	M	M	S	T
T	S	S	S	E	O	I	H	S	M	E	N	E
C	H	I	L	D	R	E	N	T	W	W	V	E
Z	E	Y	C	K	X	S	O	K	R	R	A	T
U	S	L	L	A	D	I	E	S	F	F	R	H
A	S	T	R	A	W	B	E	R	R	I	E	S

Pairwork

Work in pairs. Draw five things from this unit. Say what each thing is and if you like it or not.

Writing

Write a list of the things in your room.

Prepositions of place

| at | behind | between | in | in front of | near | next to | on | under |

We use prepositions of place to show where something or someone is located. The most common prepositions of place are:

- *at*
  She is **at** her house in the village.

- *behind*
  They live **behind** the school.

- *between*
  The bank is **between** the museum and the supermarket.

- *in*
  The birthday present is **in** the bag.

- *in front of*
  The whiteboard is **in front of** the students.

- *near*
  We live **near** the hospital.

- *next to*
  The cinema is **next to** the shopping centre.

- *on*
  The pencil is **on** the table.

- *under*
  The umbrella is **under** the chair.

There's a river.

Yes, there is. There's a bridge and there are skyscrapers, too.

1 **Complete the sentences with the words from the box.**

behind   between   in   in front of   near   ~~next to~~   on   under

1

2

3

4

5

6

7

8

1 The train is ____next to____ the box.
2 The train is _____ the box.
3 The train is _____ the table.
4 The train is _____ the station.

5 The train is _____ the bridge.
6 The train is _____ the station.
7 The yellow train is _____ the blue train and the green train.
8 The train is _____ the car.

On, in, at

There are some useful phrases with prepositions of place.

- *on*
  on the plane/train/bus
  on the left/right
  on the wall

- *in*
  in bed
  in hospital
  in a car
  in the middle
  in an armchair

- *at*
  at school
  at work
  at home
  at the top
  at the bottom

2 **Find the mistakes in the sentences. Then write them correctly.**

1 There is a painting <u>in</u> the wall.
   There is a painting on the wall.

2 They are in home today.
   _____

3 There are five people at the car.
   _____

4 The house is at the right.
   _____

5 Grandma sits on her armchair.
   _____

6 The children are at their bikes now.
   _____

7 The table is on the middle of the kitchen.
   _____

8 There are strange animals in the bottom of the sea.
   _____

There is/there are

Affirmative	Negative	Question
there is (there's)	there is not (there isn't)	Is there?
there are	there are not (there aren't)	Are there?

Short answers	
Yes, there is.	No, there isn't.
Yes, there are.	No, there aren't.

We use *there is* and *there are* to talk or ask about what exists when we are describing something in the present.

There is a boat on the lake.
There are two people in the car.
There aren't any big houses here.
Are there three people in the photograph?

Think about it!

We use *there is* for singular nouns and *there are* for plural nouns.

3 Circle the correct answer.

1 *There is /* There are hundreds of cars on the roads.
2 *There is / There are* a post office in the village.
3 *There is / There are* two books on the chair.
4 *There is / There are* kangaroos at the zoo.
5 *There is / There are* a baby in the family.
6 *There is / There are* a bike in front of the house.
7 *There is / There are* a factory near the school.
8 *There is / There are* thirty children in the classroom.

4 Answer the questions.

1 Is there a book on the desk? ✘
   No, there isn't.

2 Are there bananas in the bowl? ✔
   _____

3 Are there people in the school? ✘
   _____

4 Is there ice cream in the freezer? ✔
   _____

5 Is there a bus stop near here? ✘
   _____

6 Is there a computer on the table? ✔
   _____

7 Are there flowers in the garden? ✔
   _____

8 Is there an elephant at the zoo? ✘
   _____

5 **Draw a picture of a city scene. Then write sentences with *there is* and *there are*, and prepositions of place.**

1   There is a lot of traffic on the road.

2   _____

3   _____

4   _____

5   _____

6   _____

6 **Write questions.**

1   ruler / in / pencil case?

   Is there a ruler in the pencil case?

2   picture / next to / window?

   _____

   _____

3   cafés / near / market?

   _____

   _____

4   plates / on / table?

   _____

   _____

5   playground / in front of / school?

   _____

   _____

7 **Complete the text with the words from the box.**

behind   between   ~~in~~   middle   next   on   there (x2)

There are lots of things [1] _____in_____ Iraj's bedroom. In the [2] _____ of the room,
[3] _____ is a big bed. [4] _____ the wall, [5] _____ is a poster of
Superman. Near the window, there is a table and a chair. [6] _____ to the table, there is a
bookcase. [7] _____ the bookcase and the door, there is a big cupboard with Iraj's clothes. Iraj's
school bag is [8] _____ the door. What's your bedroom like?

Pairwork

Work in pairs. Take turns to ask and answer about your bedroom.

Is there a table in your bedroom?

Yes, there is. It's next to my bed.

Writing

Write a letter to a friend. Describe your bedroom using *there is* and *there are*, and prepositions of place.

Have got

Affirmative	Negative	Question
I have (I've) got	I have not (haven't) got	Have I got?
you have (you've) got	you have not (haven't) got	Have you got?
he has (he's) got	he has not (hasn't) got	Has he got?
she has (she's) got	she has not (hasn't) got	Has she got?
it has (it's) got	it has not (hasn't) got	Has it got?
we have (we've) got	we have not (haven't) got	Have we got?
you have (you've) got	you have not (haven't) got	Have you got?
they have (they've) got	they have not (haven't) got	Have they got?

Short answers			
Yes, I have.	No, I haven't.	Yes, it has.	No, it hasn't.
Yes, you have.	No, you haven't.	Yes, we have.	No, we haven't.
Yes, he has.	No, he hasn't.	Yes, you have.	No, you haven't.
Yes, she has.	No, she hasn't.	Yes, they have.	No, they haven't.

We use *have got*:

- to show that something belongs to someone.
  I'**ve got** a new phone.

- to describe a person, thing or animal.
  She **hasn't got** brown hair.
  The house **has got** a blue door.
  A shark **has got** sharp teeth.

- to talk about a health problem.
  He'**s got** toothache.

Have you got fruit?

Yes, I've got green and red apples and some lemons.

1 Complete the sentences with the short form of *have got*.

1 You _'ve got_____ lots of food in the fridge.

2 They _____ a house in the countryside.

3 He _____ a good job.

4 She _____ two brothers.

5 I _____ a bad cough.

6 We _____ a new kite.

7 They _____ a small flat.

8 My bedroom _____ a large window.

2 Complete the sentences with the negative form of *have got*.

1 She ____hasn't got____ a pet.

2 The house _____ a big garden.

3 I _____ a black and yellow pen.

4 We _____ a house by the sea.

5 Sasha _____ a cold.

6 You _____ time for this.

7 She _____ blue eyes; she's got green eyes.

8 I _____ long hair.

3 Complete the questions with *have got* and the words in brackets.

1 ____Has the baby got_____ (the baby) dark hair?

2 _____ (you) good friends at school?

3 _____ (I) a dirty face?

4 _____ (Marta) a sore neck?

5 _____ (he) a motorbike?

6 _____ (they) tickets for the match?

7 _____ (the man) a beard?

8 _____ (shopping centre) a car park?

Think about it! ☼

In questions, we cannot use the short form.

4 Answer the questions. Give extra information if you can.

1 Have you got good transport in your town?

Yes, we have. We've got a big train station and there are lots of buses.

2 Have you got short hair?

_____

3 Have you got a headache?

_____

4 Have you got brothers and sisters?

_____

5 Have you got a bike?

_____

6 Have you got interesting hobbies?

_____

5 Complete the table with the phrases from the box. Then write questions and answers.

> a bill   a short mane   a long head   black and white feathers
> black and white stripes   four thin legs   pointed ears
> small eyes   two feet   two flippers (wings)

A penguin has got	A zebra has got
a bill	

1 Has a penguin got a bill?

   Yes, it has.

2 _____

   _____

3 _____

   _____

4 _____

   _____

5 _____

   _____

6 _____

   _____

7 _____

   _____

8 _____

   _____

9 _____

   _____

10 _____

   _____

6 Write the words in the correct order.

1 has / long / it / a / tail / got

   It has got a long tail.

2 hasn't / red / he / jacket / got / a

   _____

3 a piece of cake / got / have / you / ?

   _____

4 four / they / got / children / haven't

   _____

5 Rahul / big / got / has / moustache / a / ?

   _____

6 I / sore / foot / got / a / have

   _____

7 **Rewrite the sentences using the full form.**

1 It's a hot day.
   It is a hot day.

2 Tina's got a lot of clothes.
   _____

3 The boy's in the classroom.
   _____

4 There's a strange person outside.
   _____

5 Look at the cake. It's got fruit on it. Yummy!
   _____

6 She's got a headache.
   _____

7 He's my best friend.
   _____

8 Milo's got two brothers and a sister.
   _____

Think about it!

She's a tall girl. = She is a tall girl.

She's got a tall sister. = She has got a tall sister.

8 **Complete the text with the correct form of *have got*.**

My name's Mia. I ¹ _____ have got _____ (✔) a brother and a sister. My brother is fifteen and my
sister is seven. I ² _____ (✔) lots of comic books and some video games. My sister
³ _____ (✔) five dolls and lots of games. She ⁴ _____ (✘) a bike. My brother
⁵ _____ (✔) a phone, but he ⁶ _____ (✘) his own tablet. I ⁷ _____ (✔)
a computer, but I ⁸ _____ (✘) a camera. My mum and dad ⁹ _____ (✔) a big car
and a small house by the sea. We ¹⁰ _____ (✔) a pet cat called Miaow.

Pairwork

**Work in pairs. Take turns to ask and answer about what you have or haven't got.
Then tell your partner what the members of your family have or haven't got.**

What have you got?

What has your sister got?

I have got a pet fish. I haven't got a cat.

She's got a lot of books.

Writing

Write a paragraph about yourself. Include the points below.

- what you have got
- what you haven't got

1 **Complete the sentences with the present simple of _to be_.**

1 The café _____is_____ open now. ✔

2 The river _____ near our house. ✗

3 The pens _____ on the desk. ✗

4 James and Monica _____ good friends. ✔

5 He _____ very happy today. ✗

6 My grandma _____ one hundred years old! ✔

7 I _____ thirsty now. ✗

8 The trees in the forest _____ very green. ✔

2 **Complete the questions with _am_, _are_ or _is_. Then answer the questions.**

1 _____Is_____ dinner ready? ✔

____Yes, it is._____

2 _____ the taxi at the door? ✗

_____

3 _____ we nearly home? ✗

_____

4 _____ the boys in the garden? ✔

_____

5 _____ you at work now? ✔

_____

6 _____ the shoes under the bed? ✗

_____

7 _____ the bed next to the window? ✔

_____

8 _____ you ill? ✗

_____

3 **Circle the correct answer.**

1 _They_ / _She_ is English.

2 Are _she_ / _they_ in the car?

3 _We_ / _He_ aren't in the house.

4 _He_ / _I_ isn't in the garden.

5 _I_ / _She_ am a teacher.

6 Are _you_ / _I_ tired?

7 _We_ / _I_ are hungry.

8 _He_ / _I_ is at the gym.

4 **Write sentences and questions with _to be_.**

1 our friends / be / at the cinema now

____Our friends are at the cinema now.____

2 your sister / be / ready for school / ?

_____

3 Yakob / be / very kind

_____

4 Miss Bal / not be / at the office now

_____

5 you / be / sad today / ?

_____

6 the sea / be / very cold

_____

7 he / not be / very strong

_____

8 the keys / be / in her bag

_____

5 **Complete the table with the words from the box.**

ant   apple   bag   banana   cat   elephant   funny story   happy girl
hour   house   insect   interesting day   orange jacket   unhappy boy
wet dog   yellow chair

a	an
bag	ant

6 **Write the plurals.**

Singular	Plural
1 watch	watches
2 tooth	_____
3 photo	_____
4 sheep	_____
5 man	_____
6 bus	_____
7 fox	_____
8 brush	_____
9 woman	_____
10 boy	_____
11 person	_____
12 child	_____
13 mouse	_____
14 foot	_____
15 party	_____

7 **Complete the sentences with *there is* or *there are*.**

1 ___There are___ two sports centres in our town.

2 _____ a car in the street.

3 _____ a supermarket near the school.

4 _____ twenty students in our class.

5 _____ a nice restaurant on this street.

6 _____ hundreds of apples on the tree.

7 _____ five books in the bag.

8 _____ a bird in my garden.

8 **Write questions and answers with *there is* or *there are*.**

1 a blue pen / on / the desk / ? ✔

  <u>Is there a blue pen on the desk?</u>

  <u>Yes, there is.</u>

2 two oranges / on / the table / ? ✘

3 a big park / opposite / your school / ? ✘

4 a black bag / under / the chair / ? ✔

5 pencils / in / the drawer / ? ✘

6 a whiteboard / in / the classroom / ? ✔

7 a small tree / in / his garden / ? ✘

8 nice restaurants / near / the sea / ? ✔

9 **Find the mistakes in the sentences. Then write them correctly.**

1 Dad isn't <u>in</u> work today.

  <u>Dad isn't at work today.</u>

2 The students are not in school now.

3 There are six people in the bus stop.

4 It's the third house at the right.

5 Her parents sit on their armchairs every day.

6 The picture is on the top of the page.

7 Mum is in home.

8 My sister's room is in my room and the bathroom.

10 **Complete the sentences with prepositions of place.**

1

2

3

4

5

6

1 The ball is _____next to_____ the chair.

2 The ball is _____ the chair

3 The ball is _____ the chair.

4 The ball is _____ the chair.

5 The ball is _____ the two chairs.

6 The ball is _____ the chair.

11 **Complete the sentences with *have got*. Use the short form.**

1 I _'ve got_____ a new bike. ✔

2 I _____ a headache. ✔

3 We _____ a house by the sea. ✗

4 They _____ a beautiful garden. ✔

5 I _____ a new coat. ✗

6 You _____ good grades. ✔

7 She _____ a brother or a sister. ✗

8 We _____ three grandparents. ✔

12 **Complete the questions with *have got* and the words in brackets.**

1 _____Has Mr Evans got_____ (Mr Evans) a new car?

2 _____ (they) tickets for the cinema?

3 _____ (you) a tablet?

4 _____ (Susan) a headache?

5 _____ (the baby) curly hair?

6 _____ (you) family in Australia?

7 _____ (I) paint on my face?

8 _____ (the boy) a sore throat?

Possessives, *who's ...?* and *whose ...?*

Possessive adjectives

Subject pronouns	Possessive adjectives
I	my
you	your
he	his
she	her
it	its
we	our
you	your
they	their

We use possessive adjectives when:
- something belongs to someone.
  *This is **my** car.*
- someone has a particular relationship with someone or something.
  *Gonzalo is **her** brother.*

Notes

We don't use *the* or *a* with possessive adjectives.
***My** bike is in the garden.*
***The** bike is in the garden.*
***A** bike is in the garden.*

Think about it!

The possessive adjective *its* does not have an apostrophe. *It's* means *it is*.

---

1 **Complete the sentences with possessive adjectives.**

1 _____Its_____ (it) food is in the bowl.

2 _____ (you) bag is here.

3 _____ (they) house is next to the café.

4 _____ (we) car is blue.

5 _____ (he) sister is my best friend.

6 _____ (you) garden is lovely!

7 _____ (she) trainers are red.

8 _____ (you) bikes are fast.

> Whose flat is that?

> It's ours! It's our new home! And these are our keys.

Possessive *'s*

We use *'s* to show that something belongs to someone.
They are Karl's books.

We add *'s* to names or to singular nouns.
Jenna's father has got a good job.
The girl's mother has got a good job.

When the noun is plural, we add an apostrophe.
The girls' mothers have got good jobs.

When the noun has an irregular plural, we add *'s*.
The children's mothers have got good jobs.

2 **Complete the sentences with the possessive *'s* (*'s* or *'*) and the word in brackets.**

1 ____Nadia's____ (Nadia) phone is on the table.
2 My _____ (cousin) name is Annam.
3 His _____ (father) car is a Honda.
4 The _____ (boys) pet is called Boris.
5 Their _____ (friend) house is near our house.
6 The _____ (head teacher) room is on the right.
7 His _____ (brothers) names are Rafa and Pablo.
8 The _____ (men) clothes are very expensive.

Possessive pronouns

Possessive adjectives		Possessive pronouns	
my	its	mine	–
your	our	yours	ours
his	your	his	your
her	their	hers	theirs

We use possessive pronouns when something belongs to someone or when someone has a particular relationship with something.
*The bag is **hers**.*

After a possessive adjective, there is always a noun. A possessive pronoun replaces a possessive adjective and a noun.
*It's her **bag**.* → *It's **hers**.*
*It's my **book**.* → *The book is **mine**.*

3 **Complete the sentences with possessive pronouns.**

1 The brown tent is (he) _____his_____ .
2 The blue pencil is (you) _____ .
3 The coffee is (she) _____ .
4 The house is (they) _____ .
5 The money is (you) _____ .
6 The sandwiches are (we) _____ .

Demonstratives

Singular	Plural
this	these
that	those

We use demonstratives to show that something or someone is near us (*this, these*) or further away (*that, those*).
This is my bag. **That** bag is yours.
These pens are Sienna's. **Those** are Hilda's pens.

When we want to ask a question, we use the verb *to be*.
Is this your book? **Is this** book yours?
Are these Sienna's pencils? **Are these** pencils Sienna's?

4 **Write sentences with *this, that, these* or *those*.**

1 apples

2 bananas

3 sandwich

4 cake

5 eggs

6 ice cream

7 glass

8 books

1 <u>These are apples.</u>
2 _____
3 _____
4 _____

5 _____
6 _____
7 _____
8 _____

Who's …? and Whose …?

Don't confuse *Who's …?* and *Whose …?*
Who's …? means *Who is …?*
Who's at the door? (**Who is** at the door?)

Whose …? asks who something belongs to.
Whose is this key?
Whose shoes are these?

5 **Circle the correct answer.**

1 *Who's* / (*Whose*) pens are these?
2 *Who's* / *Whose* on the phone?
3 *Who's* / *Whose* outside?
4 *Who's* / *Whose* are those books?
5 *Who's* / *Whose* ticket is this?
6 *Who's* / *Whose* at home?

6 **Rewrite the sentences.**

1   Those are his trousers.
    They're his.

2   This is her pet.
    _____

3   That is their car.
    _____

4   Those are our sandwiches.
    _____

5   That is my English book.
    _____

6   These are your video games.
    _____

7   This is our new house.
    _____

8   Those are your clothes.
    _____

9   Those are my trainers.
    _____

10 Those are their phones.
    _____

Think about it!

We can say:

Whose is this drink? or *Whose drink is this?*

---

7 **Circle the correct answer.**

1   Is this your car? Yes, it's ___ .
    a   our   b   we   c   ours

2   This phone is ___ .
    a   Juan's   b   Juans'   c   Juan

3   ___ apples are green.
    a   That   b   Mine   c   Those

4   The books are ___ .
    a   they   b   theirs   c   their

5   ___ parents have got a shop.
    a   Hers   b   Her   c   Whose

6   ___ Ella's clothes?
    a   Are these   b   These are   c   Is this

Pairwork

Work in pairs. Find five objects and put them in front of you. Take turns to talk about all the objects.

This is my pen. It's mine.

This is your book. It's yours.

Writing

Write ten sentences or questions about yourself, your family and your friends using the language from this unit.

Present simple

Affirmative	Negative	Question
I want	I do not (don't) want	Do I want?
you want	you do not (don't) want	Do you want?
he wants	he does not (doesn't) want	Does he want?
she wants	she does not (doesn't) want	Does she want?
it wants	it does not (doesn't) want	Does it want?
we want	we do not (don't) want	Do we want?
you want	you do not (don't) want	Do you want?
they want	they do not (don't) want	Do they want?

Short answers

Yes, I do.	No, I don't.	Yes, it does.	No, it doesn't.
Yes, you do.	No, you don't.	Yes, we do.	No, we don't.
Yes, he does.	No, he doesn't.	Yes, you do.	No, you don't.
Yes, she does.	No, she doesn't.	Yes, they do.	No, they don't.

We use the present simple to talk about:

- permanent states.
  *My sister **lives** in Brazil.*

- things we do often.
  *He **visits** his grandparents every weekend.*

- general truths.
  *It **gets** hot in Spain in the summer.*

Do you want pasta or pizza?

I don't want pasta. I want pizza, please!

In the third person singular affirmative (*he, she, it*), we add *-s* to the verb.

find → *find**s***   *laugh* → *laugh**s***

We add *-es* to verbs which end in *-ss, -sh, -ch, -x* and *-o* in the third person singular affirmative.

press → *press**es***   *wash* → *wash**es***
watch → *watch**es***   *fix* → *fix**es***
do → *does*

When a verb ends in a consonant + *-y*, we take off the *-y* and add *-ies* in the third person singular affirmative.

tidy → *tid**ies***   *marry* → *marr**ies***

When a verb ends in a vowel + *-y*, we just add *-s* in the third person singular affirmative.

say → *say**s***

In the negative and question forms, we use the auxiliary verb *do/does* and the main verb in the infinitive (without *to*).

*They **don't swim** in the winter.*
*David **doesn't like** spaghetti.*
***Do** you **work** on Saturdays?*
***Does** Helen **go** to school on Sundays?*

In short answers, we only use *do/does*. We don't use the main verb.

*Do you like the theatre? Yes, I **do**.*
*Does he eat fish? No, he **doesn't**.*

1 **Complete the table.**

Verb	3rd person singular
buy	buys
do	
fix	
fly	
live	
miss	
know	
play	
wash	
write	

2 **Complete the sentences with the negative form of the present simple.**

1 They ____don't play____ (play) baseball.
2 He _____ (teach) history.
3 We _____ (watch) a lot of TV.
4 She _____ (go) to the cinema.
5 You _____ (eat) a lot of fruit.
6 I _____ (speak) Spanish.
7 She _____ (ride) a bike to work.
8 He _____ (drink) cola.

3 **Complete the questions with the present simple. Then answer the questions.**

1 ____Does he know____ (he / know) how to spell the words? ✔
   ____Yes, he does.____

2 _____ (they / eat) meat? ✗
   _____

3 _____ (I / look) nice? ✔
   _____

4 _____ (she / play) tennis? ✗
   _____

5 _____ (you / write) emails to them? ✔
   _____

6 _____ (they / buy) a lot of clothes? ✗
   _____

7 _____ (that woman / drive) a big car? ✔
   _____

8 _____ (your son / cook) well? ✗
   _____

Adverbs of frequency

When we talk about habits or we want to say how often something happens, we use adverbs of frequency. The adverbs of frequency are:

| *never* | *rarely* | *sometimes* | *often* | *usually* | *always* |

0% ←——————————————————————————————→ 100%

Adverbs of frequency usually come before the main verb, unless the verb is *to be*.
I **often go** to the cinema.
He **is usually** late for work.

Time expressions such as *every day, every week, once a week, on Mondays*, etc. usually go at the beginning or the end of a sentence.
He walks to work **every day**.
On Mondays, she plays basketball.

4 **Write the words in the correct order.**

1 late / they / for dinner / never / are
   They are never late for dinner.

2 Tom / wears / usually / jeans
   _____

3 take us / our parents / sometimes / to school / by car
   _____

4 wear / that silly hat / you / do / always / ?
   _____

5 Carlos / in the summer / often / salads / makes
   _____

6 usually / I / not / have / at this time / breakfast / do
   _____

7 busy / the doctor / always / is / ?
   _____

8 not / our parents / go swimming / do / often
   _____

Prepositions of time

At	On	In
at night	on 5th May	in June
at six o'clock	on Monday mornings	in 1987
at the weekend	on my birthday	in the afternoon
	on Saturdays	in the evening
	on World Book Day	in the holidays
		in the morning
		in the winter

5 **Complete the sentences with *at, on* or *in*.**

1   She goes to the beach every day _____in_____ the holidays.

2   He plays table tennis _____ Sundays.

3   I have an English lesson _____ seven o'clock _____ the evening.

4   We don't usually go on holiday _____ the winter.

5   They often go to the cinema _____ the weekend.

6   My birthday is _____ 13th February.

7   She always swims _____ the summer.

8   He wakes up early _____ Saturday mornings and goes shopping.

9   Do you go to bed late _____ night?

10 I never have a big party _____ my birthday.

6 **Write sentences and questions with the present simple.**

1   my parents / not go / to work / Sundays

My parents do not go to work

on Sundays.

2   my brother / never / eat / fish

_____

_____

3   teacher / always / help / his students / ?

_____

_____

4   we / play / tennis / the weekend

_____

_____

5   my sister / sometimes / watch TV / the evenings

_____

_____

6   My grandparents / often / clean / the house / Fridays

_____

_____

7 **Complete the sentences and questions with one word in each gap.**

1   I _____do_____ not like strawberry ice cream.

2   The children have maths lessons _____ Mondays and Wednesdays.

3   We have cereal and milk for breakfast _____ day.

4   _____ your best friend live near you?

5   They do _____ usually go out on Sunday evenings.

6   The sun is very hot _____ the summer.

7   Peter _____ not work in a bank.

8   Do you watch TV late _____ night?

8 **Write the words in the correct order.**

1 on holiday / go / they / never / January / in

   They never go on holiday in January.

2 Saturdays / goes / usually / she / on / out / with her friends

   _____

3 they / noodles / eat / do / often / ?

   _____

4 have / doesn't / the / at / she / English lessons / weekend

   _____

5 sometimes / see / I / my cousins / after school

   _____

6 see / he / every / doesn't / his best friend / week

   _____

9 **Find the mistakes in the sentences and questions. Then write them correctly.**

1 <u>You</u> want an ice cream?

   <u>Do you want an ice cream?</u>

2 They not go on holiday every year.

   _____

3 Do he often go to the gym?

   _____

4 He is catches the train every day.

   _____

5 They finish school on June.

   _____

6 She don't want pizza today.

   _____

10 **Complete the text with the present simple.**

My big brother [1] _____is_____ (be) funny. He [2] _____ (like) tennis, but he
[3] _____ (not like) table tennis. He [4] _____ (not eat) healthy food,
but he [5] _____ (be) very thin. He [6] _____ (not study) a lot, but he
[7] _____ (get) good marks at university. He [8] _____ (not tidy) his room,
but he [9] _____ (tidy) his desk. He [10] _____ (talk) a lot, but he often
[11] _____ (want) to be quiet and read a book. I [12] _____ (not understand)
my brother, but he [13] _____ (love) me and I [14] _____ (love) him a lot!

11 **Complete the sentences and questions with the present simple.**

1 _____*Do*_____ you _____*study*_____ (study) every day?

2 He often _____ (watch) football on TV.

3 They _____ (not go) to the gym on Sundays.

4 _____ she _____ (read) a lot of books?

5 He usually _____ (catch) the train at seven o'clock.

6 _____ they _____ (visit) their friends often?

7 I _____ (not go) running, but I go swimming.

8 She _____ (not like) fruit, but she likes vegetables.

> **Think about it!**
>
> We can put the word *often* at the end of question.

Pairwork

Work in pairs. Take turns to ask and answer the questions below.

- Do you live in a flat or a house?
- Have you got any brothers or sisters?
- What do you do in the mornings?
- What do you do in the evenings?
- What do you do in your free time?

- Do you like music?
- Do you play the piano?
- Do you like sport?
- Do you play football?
- Do you read lots?

Writing

Write a paragraph about your partner using his or her answers from the questions above.

Adverbs, *too* and *enough*

Work hard, play hard, eat healthily and sleep well.

Adverbs

Adjectives	Adverbs
bad	badly
careful	carefully
nice	nicely
noisy	noisily
simple	simply
soft	softly

Adjectives	Adverbs
early	early
fast	fast
good	well
hard	hard
late	late

Adverbs describe how we do something.
She drives her car **carefully***.*

We usually make adverbs by adding *-ly*
to the adjective.
quick → *quick**ly***
helpful → *helpful**ly***

When the adjective ends in *-y*, we take off
the *-y* and add *-ily.*
easy → *eas**ily***

When the adjective ends in *-le*, we take off
the *-e* and add *-y.*
simple → *simp**ly***

Some adverbs don't end in *-ly* and have
the same form as the adjective.
hard → **hard**   *fast* → **fast**
early → **early**   *late* → **late**

Some adverbs don't end in *-ly* and have
a different form from the adjective.
good → **well**

Adverbs that describe how we do
something usually go after the main verb.
He **runs quickly** *around the park
every morning.*

34

1 **Complete the table.**

Adjectives	Adverbs
angry	angrily
dangerous	
good	
happy	
hard	
heavy	
light	
polite	
quick	
quiet	
sad	
slow	
terrible	
useful	

2 **Complete the sentences with adverbs.**

1 He talks very ____quickly____ (quick) when he's on the phone.

2 Please play _____ (quiet), children. I've got a headache.

3 She does very _____ (good) in her exams.

4 Drive _____ (careful) on your way home!

5 The teacher talks _____ (slow).

6 I run _____ (fast).

7 I usually get up _____ (late) on Sundays.

8 Those children speak _____ (polite).

9 The little boy plays _____ (happy) with his toys every day.

10 My dad sings _____ (loud) in the shower.

11 She plays the piano _____ (bad).

12 They ride their bikes _____ (danger).

Too and *enough*

Too has a negative meaning. It means very much, or more than is necessary or wanted.
*I can't lift that box. It's **too** heavy.*

We usually use the word *too* to say that someone is *too small, big, slow,* etc. to do something. We use:

too + adjective/adverb + *to* + verb.
*She's **too young to go** to a nightclub.*

Enough has a positive meaning. It means as many/much as is necessary or wanted. It goes before a noun but after an adjective or adverb.
*There are **enough chairs** in the room.*
*She's **clever enough** to pass her exam.*
*He can win the race. He's **fast enough**.*

We often use the word *enough* to say that someone or something is *small, big, slow,* etc. enough to do something. We use:

adjective/adverb + *enough* + *to* + verb
*It's **warm enough to go** swimming today.*

enough + noun + *to* + verb.
*I've got **enough money to buy** a game.*

3 **Complete the sentences with *too* and the words in brackets.**

1 I'm ____too hungry to wait____ (hungry / wait) for lunch.

2 It's _____ (cold / have) a picnic.

3 They're _____ (polite / say) 'no'.

4 The exercise is (difficult / do) _____ .

5 The coat is (expensive / buy) _____ .

6 The food is (hot / eat) _____ .

7 I'm _____ (big / wear) this dress!

8 She's _____ (tired / go) out.

4 **Complete the sentences with *enough* and the words in brackets.**

1 He isn't ____calm enough to take____ (calm / take) the exam.

2 It isn't _____ (hot / go) swimming.

3 She isn't _____ (fast / win) the race.

4 The painting is _____ (good / put) on the wall.

5 The little girl isn't _____ (tall / open) the door.

6 The teenager is _____ (old / drive) a car.

5 **Complete the sentences and questions with *enough* and the words in brackets.**

1 Have you got ____enough money to buy____ (money / buy) those shoes?

2 I haven't got _____ (time / fix) the bike now.

3 There aren't _____ (snacks / give) to all the children.

4 Have they got _____ (space / have) the party at their house?

6 **Circle the correct answer.**

1 My mother is __ to come to the meeting.

   (a) too busy   b busy enough

2 The boys work very __ .

   a slow   b slowly

3 She speaks English very __ .

   a badly   b good

4 The beds are __ .

   a softly   b soft enough

5 The book is too difficult __ .

   a to read   b read

6 He plays football __ .

   a well   b good

7 **Match 1–6 with a–f. Then write sentences.**

1 The children shout   a beautifully.
2 It's raining too hard   b to go for a walk.
3 There isn't enough   c fast along this road.
4 People drive   d every Saturday.
5 She sings   e loudly at break time.
6 He plays basketball   f juice for all our friends.

1 The children shout loudly at break time.
2 _____
3 _____
4 _____
5 _____
6 _____

Think about it!

He works very hard. = He works a lot.
He works too hard. = He works more than he should.

Pairwork

Work in pairs. Take turns to ask and answer the questions below.

- Do you get up early or late on work/school days?
- Do you go to bed early or late on work/school days?
- Do you get up early or late at the weekend?
- Do you go to bed early or late at the weekend?
- Do you play football well or badly?
- Do you sing beautifully?
- Do you ride your bike carefully or carelessly?
- Do you speak English well or badly?

Writing

Write a paragraph about yourself using your answers from the questions above.

Present continuous

Affirmative	Negative	Question
I am (I'm) eating	I am not (I'm not) eating	Am I eating?
you are (you're) eating	you are not (aren't) eating	Are you eating?
he is (he's) eating	he is not (isn't) eating	Is he eating?
she is (she's) eating	she is not (isn't) eating	Is she eating?
it is (it's) eating	it is not (isn't) eating	Is it eating?
we are (we're) eating	we are not (aren't) eating	Are we eating?
you are (you're) eating	you are not (aren't) eating	Are you eating?
they are (they're) eating	they are not (aren't) eating	Are they eating?

Short answers

Yes, I am.	No, I'm not.	Yes, it is.	No, it isn't.
Yes, you are.	No, you aren't.	Yes, we are.	No, we aren't.
Yes, he is.	No, he isn't.	Yes, you are.	No, you aren't.
Yes, she is.	No, she isn't.	Yes, they are.	No, they aren't.

What are you doing?

I'm drawing a picture for my friend.

We use the present continuous to talk about:
- things that are in progress at the time of speaking.
  *What **are** they do**ing**?*
  *They**'re** eat**ing** their lunch.*
- things that are in progress around the time of speaking or that are temporary.
  *He**'s** look**ing** for a new flat.*

The present continuous is formed with *am/are/is* and the main verb with the *-ing* ending.
jump → *jump**ing***
*She's so excited, she**'s** jump**ing** up and down.*

When the main verb ends in *-e*, we take off the *-e* and add *-ing*.
make → *mak**ing***

When the verb ends in a consonant and before that consonant there is a vowel, we double the final consonant and add *-ing*.
win → *win**ning***

When the verb ends in *-l*, we double the *-l* and add *-ing*.
cancel → *cancel**ling***

When the verb ends in *-ie*, we take off the *-ie* and add *-y* and *-ing*.
tie → *t**ying***   *lie* → *l**ying***   *die* → *d**ying***

Notes

We can use time expressions such as *now, at the moment, these days, at present, today,* etc. with the present continuous.
*He**'s** wash**ing** his car **at the moment**.*

---

1 | **Write the *-ing* form of the verbs. Then complete the table.**

1 carry ___carrying___
2 close _____
3 come _____
4 draw _____
5 drive _____
6 get _____

7 give _____
8 go _____
9 leave _____
10 open _____
11 play _____
12 put _____

13 ride _____
14 run _____
15 sit _____
16 stop _____
17 study _____
18 swim _____

hit → hitting	write → writing	work → working
		carrying

Think about it!

My mum's working today. = My mum is at work today.

My mum's name is Lydia. = The name of my mother is Lydia.

2 Complete the sentences with the present continuous.

1 They ___are writing___ (write) text messages to their friends.

2 Dad _____ (get) lunch ready.

3 The boys _____ (ride) their bikes in the street.

4 I _____ (talk) to my cousin at the moment.

5 Grandma _____ (sit) in the garden.

6 The children _____ (study) hard for the test.

7 She _____ (learn) how to use her new computer.

8 We _____ (live) in Japan at present.

3 Complete the sentences with negative form of the present continuous.

1 They _____are not listening_____ (listen) to the news.

2 She _____ (work) very hard.

3 We _____ (have) fish for lunch.

4 It _____ (snow) today.

5 I _____ (make) breakfast now.

6 The babies _____ (sleep) at the moment.

7 He _____ (help) to clean the house today.

8 You _____ (do) any work. Come and help me!

4 Complete the questions with the present continuous. Then answer the questions.

1 ___Is the baby boy smiling___ (the baby boy / smile) at you? ✔

   ___Yes, he is.___

2 _____ (you / have) a good time? ✔

   _____

3 _____ (the students / do) the exercise? ✘

   _____

4 _____ (he / eat) at the moment? ✘

   _____

5 _____ (they / wait) for the bus? ✔

   _____

6 _____ (it / rain) outside? ✘

   _____

7 _____ (you / leave) now? ✘

   _____

8 _____ (your sister / play) on your computer? ✔

   _____

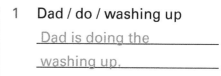

5 **Write sentences with the present continuous.**

1 Dad / do / washing up
  Dad is doing the
  washing up.

2 the cat / drink / milk
  _____
  _____

3 the children / cycle / to school
  _____
  _____

4 the family / have / a picnic
  _____
  _____

5 we / swim / in a pool
  _____
  _____

6 they / run / by the river
  _____
  _____

7 she / drive / her car
  _____
  _____

8 he / make / his bed
  _____
  _____

Pairwork

Work in pairs. It is eight o'clock on a Saturday evening. Your partner, your partner's family and a few friends are at his/her house. Ask your partner what everyone is doing.

Writing

Write a short email to a friend. Include the points below.

* what you are doing at the moment
* what the weather is like
* what the members of your family are doing

1 **Complete the table.**

Subject pronouns	Possessive adjectives	Possessive pronouns
I	my	mine
you		
he		
she		
it		
we		
you		
they		

2 **Complete the sentences with possessive pronouns.**

1   They're your cakes. They're _____yours_____ .

2   They're our pencils. They're _____ .

3   They're his jeans. They're _____ .

4   It's her bag. It's _____ .

5   It's his computer. It's _____ .

6   They're my toys. They're _____ .

7   It's her milkshake. It's _____ .

8   It's their piano. It's _____ .

3 **Complete the sentences with possessive adjectives.**

1   _____His_____ (he) sister is my best friend.

2   _____ (you) new coat is very nice.

3   _____ (she) shoes are black.

4   _____ (it) arms are long.

5   _____ (she) juice is over there.

6   _____ (I) camera is new.

7   _____ (they) house is next to the school.

8   _____ (we) bikes are fast.

4 Complete the sentences with the present simple.

1 You _____eat_____ (eat) a lot of vegetables.

2 Jasiek _____ (not speak) Spanish.

3 My parents _____ (not go) to work by bus.

4 Helena _____ (drink) a glass of water every morning.

5 My friends _____ (not play) computer games.

6 She _____ (teach) geography.

7 Suli and I _____ (buy) a lot of clothes every year.

8 We _____ (not live) in a village.

5 Complete the questions with the present simple. Then answer the questions.

1 _____Do you see_____ (you / see) your grandparents every month? ✔

_Yes, I do._____

2 _____ (they / know) a lot of people? ✗

_____

3 _____ (Siya / often / tidy) her bedroom? ✔

_____

4 _____ (Danny / always / cook) nice meals? ✔

_____

5 _____ (he / usually / listen) to music? ✗

_____

6 _____ (the parrot / eat) a lot of fruit? ✔

_____

7 _____ (you / want) an ice cream? ✗

_____

8 _____ (she / drive) a blue car? ✔

_____

6 Circle the correct answer.

1 (In)/ At winter, we go skiing.

2 They often go out for a meal on / at the weekend.

3 His birthday is at / in September.

4 She goes to the beach on / in the summer.

5 I open my presents early on / at my birthday.

6 He goes shopping at / on Saturdays.

7 I usually have a maths lesson to / at five o'clock.

8 He travels a lot at / in the holidays.

7 **Complete the sentences with _too_ and the words in brackets.**

1   The jacket is _____too old to wear_____ (old / wear).

2   The pasta is _____ (hot / eat).

3   The books are _____ (heavy / carry).

4   She's _____ (busy / visit) her friends.

5   It's _____ (wet / go) out.

6   He's _____ (young / understand).

7   The song is _____ (difficult / learn).

8   It's _____ (cold / have) a picnic.

8 **Complete the table.**

Adjectives	Adverbs
angry	angrily
beautiful	
easy	
fast	
good	
happy	
hard	
heavy	
horrible	
late	
light	
polite	
quick	
quiet	
simple	
slow	

9 **Rewrite the sentences using the word in bold.**

1   The soup is too hot to eat. **cool**

The soup _____is not cool enough_____ to eat.

2   The babies are not old enough to talk. **young**

The babies _____ .

3   I am too short to reach the top shelf. **tall**

I am _____ to reach the top shelf.

4   The bed is too hard for me. **soft**

The bed _____ for me.

5   The bag is too heavy to lift easily. **light**

The bag _____ to lift easily.

6   The girl is too slow to win the race. **fast**

The girl _____ to win the race.

10 **Complete the sentences and questions with *enough* and the words in brackets.**

1 There aren't _enough good programmes to watch_ (good programmes / watch) on TV.
2 Have you got _____ (money / buy) that video game?
3 I haven't got _____ (time / check) your homework now.
4 We've got _____ (sandwiches / give) to all the children.
5 There isn't _____ (cheese / put) in the pasta.
6 Has she got _____ (eggs / make) a cake?

11 **Complete the sentences and questions with the present continuous.**

1 They ___are writing___ (write) an email to their cousins in the US.
2 _____ Mum _____ (get) breakfast ready?
3 They _____ (not listen) to music.
4 The girl _____ (take) out the rubbish.
5 We _____ (not have) salad for lunch.
6 It _____ (not rain) today.
7 I _____ (paint) a mountain.
8 She _____ (not work) late tonight.

12 **Complete the questions with the present continuous. Then answer the questions.**

1 _Are the people running_ (the people / run) for the bus? ✔
   Yes, they are.

2 _____ (it / snow) outside? ✗
   _____

3 _____ (you / study) at the moment? ✔
   _____

4 _____ (your friend / play) on the computer? ✗
   _____

5 _____ (the baby / sleep) ? ✗
   _____

6 _____ (you / have) a party? ✗
   _____

7 _____ (Ms Harris / mark) the students' homework? ✔
   _____

8 _____ (they / stay) at home ? ✗
   _____

Present simple and present continuous

	Affirmative	Negative	Question
Present simple	I eat he eats	I do not (don't) eat he does not (doesn't) eat	Do I eat? Does he eat?
Present continuous	I am (I'm) eating he is (he's) eating	I am not (I'm not) eating he is not (he isn't) eating	Am I eating? Is he eating?

We use the present simple to talk about:

* permanent situations.
  *My brother **works** in London.*
* habits.
  *I **practise** the piano **every day**.*
* general truths.
  *Lions **eat** meat.*

We use the present continuous to talk about:

* things that are in progress at the time we are speaking.
  *She's mak**ing** lunch **now**.*
* things that are in progress around the time of speaking or that are temporary.
  *They**'re** paint**ing** their bedroom **at the moment**.*

Every day, we go to school by bus.

But today, we aren't going to school. We're going on a trip!

Time expressions

We often use adverbs of frequency (*never*, *sometimes*, *often*, *usually*, *always*) and time expressions such as *at the weekend, on Saturdays, every day, in the mornings, in the summer*, etc. with the present simple.
He **usually leaves** for work **at eleven o'clock**.
They **go** for long walks **at the weekend**.

We often use time expressions such as *now, at the moment, these days, at present, this term, this year, tonight*, etc. with the present continuous.
I **am** watch**ing** the news **at the moment**.
He**'s** work**ing** very hard **this term**.

1 Complete the sentences and questions with the present simple.

1 They ___do not like___ (not like) very hot weather.

2 _____ you _____ (know) that boy over there?

3 She _____ (run) very fast.

4 _____ he _____ (live) in South Africa?

5 They _____ (not have) English lessons on Fridays.

6 She _____ (not like) coffee.

7 _____ you _____ (speak) Japanese?

8 They _____ (always travel) by train.

2 Complete the sentences and questions with the present continuous.

1 _____Are_____ they ___learning___ (learn) Spanish or Italian?

2 She _____ (not cook) dinner this evening.

3 The children _____ (draw) pictures of fruit and vegetables.

4 I _____ (watch) a film on TV.

5 He _____ (do) puzzles at the moment.

6 _____ Isabel _____ (visit) her friends?

7 The students _____ (not work) hard this term.

8 I _____ (not write) an email.

3 Complete the table with the phrases from the box.

| always   at present   at the moment   every day   in the winter   now |
| often   on Sundays   this month   this term   this year   usually |

Present simple	Present continuous
always	

4 **Write sentences with the present simple and the present continuous.**

1 Leo / usually / go for a run / seven o'clock / but today he / make pancakes for breakfast

 Leo usually goes for a run at
 seven o'clock, but today he is making
 pancakes for breakfast.

2 Leo / usually / leave for work / eight o'clock / but this morning he / water the plants / in his garden

_____

_____

_____

3 Leo / usually / have lunch at his desk / but today he / have lunch with his parents / at a café

_____

_____

_____

4 Leo / usually / read a book / in bed / but tonight he / watch a film / in his living room

_____

_____

_____

5 Complete the sentences and questions with the present simple or present continuous.

1   He never _____works_____ (work) on Saturdays.

2   _____ the sun _____ (shine) at the moment?

3   They _____ (always / not travel) by car.

4   She's got a headache and she _____ (lie) down.

5   I _____ (often / see) my friends at the weekend.

6   She _____ (not start) her new job this week.

7   We _____ (give) flowers to our mum on Mother's Day.

8   _____ he _____ (want) to go on the school trip?

6 Circle the correct answer.

1   Look! She *runs* / *is running* to catch the bus.

2   We are not working *at present* / *in the mornings*. We are on holiday.

3   *Do you play* / *Are you playing* with your friend every day?

4   They are visiting their aunt *at the moment* / *on Saturdays*.

5   Every morning, she *goes* / *is going* for a run around the park.

6   Do you go to work by bus *today* / *every day*?

7   It's cold this morning and we *wear* / *are wearing* our coats.

8   I don't come here *often* / *this afternoon*.

> **Think about it!**
>
> Don't forget that if a verb ends with one vowel and one consonant, then we double the consonant before we add *-ing*.

Pairwork

Work in pairs. Take turns to ask and answer about what you usually do at the weekend.

What do you usually do on Saturday?

I usually go swimming in the morning.

Writing

Write a paragraph about yourself. Include the points below.

*   what you usually do at the weekend
*   what you are doing now

Can and *must*

Can for ability and permission

Affirmative	Negative	Question
I can swim	I cannot (can't) swim	Can I swim?
you can swim	you cannot (can't) swim	Can you swim?
he can swim	he cannot (can't) swim	Can he swim?
she can swim	she cannot (can't) swim	Can she swim?
it can swim	it cannot (can't) swim	Can it swim?
we can swim	we cannot (can't) swim	Can we swim?
you can swim	you cannot (can't) swim	Can you swim?
they can swim	they cannot (can't) swim	Can they swim?

Short answers

Yes, I can.	No, I can't.	Yes, it can.	No, it can't.
Yes, you can.	No, you can't.	Yes, we can.	No, we can't.
Yes, he can.	No, he can't.	Yes, you can.	No, you can't.
Yes, she can.	No, she can't.	Yes, they can.	No, they can't.

We use *can* and *can't* to talk about ability. They are followed by the infinitive (without *to*).
*I **can bake** a cake.*
*You **can play** the piano.*
***Can** he **draw**?*

We also use *can* to ask for or give permission to do something.
***Can** I stay at my friend's house at the weekend?*
*You **can** borrow my car.*

We use *can* to talk about the present and the future.
*I **can go** to the shops **now**.*
*She **can come** to our party **next week**.*

Notes

We often use *can* with verbs of feeling, such as *see, hear, smell*, etc.
***Can** you **see** the bus?*
*I **can hear** someone's phone ringing.*

I can't study any more.
I must go to bed!

1 **Complete the sentences and questions with *can* and the verb in brackets.**

1   _____Can_____ you _____run_____ (run) 100 metres?

2   They _____ (not come) to the water park on Saturday.

3   He _____ (help) me with the bags.

4   She _____ (not find) her keys.

5   _____ they _____ (ride) a unicycle?

6   I _____ (not play) the guitar.

7   We _____ (not go) on holiday this year.

8   _____ you _____ (see) the sea from the village?

2 **Complete the sentences and questions with *can* and the verb in brackets.**

1   You _____can't call_____ (not call) Grandma now. She's at work.

2   It's hot! _____ I _____ (open) the window?

3   You _____ (have) a new watch for your birthday.

4   _____ we _____ (invite) our friends for dinner on Friday?

5   _____ I _____ (watch) the match this evening?

6   You _____ (not go) out now. Do your homework, please.

7   _____ they _____ (buy) some new clothes on holiday?

8   You _____ (not stay) up late tonight. You've got school tomorrow.

3 **Write questions. Then answer the questions.**

1   you / cook a meal? ✔

   _Can you cook a meal_____ ?

   _Yes, I can._____

2   he / fix his bike? ✗

   _____ ?

   _____

3   she / speak Arabic? ✔

   _____ ?

   _____

4   you / roller skate? ✗

   _____ ?

   _____

5   we / have pancakes for lunch? ✔

   _____ ?

   _____

6   I / close the window? ✔

   _____ ?

   _____

7   they / take photos in the museum? ✗

   _____ ?

   _____

8   she / come home with us? ✔

   _____ ?

   _____

Must for obligation and prohibition

Affirmative	Negative	Question
I must go	I must not (mustn't) go	Must I go?
you must go	you must not (mustn't) go	Must you go?
he must go	he must not (mustn't) go	Must he go?
she must go	she must not (mustn't) go	Must she go?
it must go	it must not (mustn't) go	Must it go?
we must go	we must not (mustn't) go	Must we go?
you must go	you must not (mustn't) go	Must you go?
they must go	they must not (mustn't) go	Must they go?

Short answers

Yes, I must.	No, I mustn't.	Yes, it must.	No, it mustn't.
Yes, you must.	No, you mustn't.	Yes, we must.	No, we mustn't.
Yes, he must.	No, he mustn't.	Yes, you must.	No, you mustn't.
Yes, she must.	No, she mustn't.	Yes, they must.	No, they mustn't.

We use *must* to talk about obligation. *Must* is followed by the infinitive (without *to*).
*I **must go** to the dentist.*
*We **must visit** your parents this weekend.*

We use *mustn't* to talk about things we are not allowed to do (prohibition).
Mustn't is also followed by the infinitive (without *to*).
*I **mustn't be** late.*
*You **mustn't drive** too fast.*

We use *must* to talk about the present and the future.
*You **must** stop writing **now**.*
*We **must** go to the bank **tomorrow**.*

Notes

It is not very polite to use *must* when we are talking to someone we don't know well or to someone who is older than us.

4 **Complete the sentences with *must* or *mustn't*.**

1 You _____ must _____ wake up early tomorrow. ✔
2 You _____ cross the street at the traffic lights. ✔
3 You _____ park your car here. ✗
4 You _____ wear a helmet if you're on your bike. ✔
5 You _____ talk in the library. ✗
6 You _____ recycle plastic bottles. ✔
7 You _____ talk on your phone at the cinema. ✗
8 You _____ worry about your exam. ✗

5   Write sentences and questions with *must* or *mustn't*.

1   you / talk when the teacher is talking ✗
     You mustn't talk when the teacher is talking.

2   I / do my homework / now ✔
     _____

3   we / go home / soon ✔
     _____

4   you / work / this evening?
     _____

5   they / make a lot of noise ✗
     _____

6   she / forget her books ✗
     _____

7   I / eat all this food?
     _____

8   you / help me with my homework ✗
     _____

9   I / be late for school ✗
     _____

10 we / put photos on the walls ✗
     _____

Think about it!

We never put *to* after *must*.

---

6   Write questions with *must* or *can*.

1   Can they ski?
     No, they can't ski.

2   _____
     Yes, they must wear a uniform.

3   _____
     Yes, they can join the drama class.

4   _____
     Yes, he must be on time for work.

5   _____
     No, they can't use their phones in class.

Pairwork

Work in pairs. Using *can*, take turns to ask and answer about the points below.

- play an instrument
- use a computer well
- understand films in English
- fix a bike
- use an English learning app

Writing

Write a short article about your friends. Include the points below.

- what they can/can't do
- what they must/mustn't do

Let's do some yoga. Sit up.
Now, close your eyes.

Imperative

We use the imperative when:

- we give instructions.
  Write your name here.
  Take your umbrella with you; it's
  raining outside!

- we want to prevent something bad
  from happening.
  Don't touch that! It's very hot!

We form the imperative with the
infinitive (without *to*). It is the same for
when we are talking to one person as it
is when we are talking to many people.
Stand up, everyone!
Turn on the light, ***George!***
Close the door!

We form the negative imperative with
the word *don't*.
Don't run!
Don't talk in the library!

We often use the word *please* to be
more polite.
Please hold my bag.
Sit down, please.

54

1 **Complete the sentences with the verbs from the box.**

| ask | be | ~~close~~ | do | eat | look | shout | tidy |

1 _____Close_____ the window, please. I'm cold. ✔
2 Please _____ . I've got a headache. ✗
3 _____ a lot of chocolate. ✗
4 _____ the teacher if you don't understand. ✔
5 _____ all the exercises now. ✗
6 _____ your room, please. ✔
7 _____ at this photo! Isn't it funny? ✔
8 _____ sad. We'll see you again soon. ✗

Let's

We use *let's* with the infinitive (without *to*) when we want to suggest something.
Let's go to the theatre.
Let's have an ice cream!

We form the negative with the word *not*. It goes after *let's* and before the infinitive.
Let's not go out tonight.
Let's not drive. Let's walk.

2 **Complete the sentences with *let's* or *let's not* and the verbs from the box.**

| be | buy | cook | go | have | ~~watch~~ |

1 ___Let's watch___ the match tonight. ✔
2 _____ for a walk. It's raining. ✗
3 _____ a party! ✔
4 _____ late for school! ✗
5 _____ a meal for our friends. ✔
6 _____ chocolates. We can buy flowers. ✗

Object pronouns

Subject pronouns	Object pronouns
I	me
you	you
he	him
she	her
it	it
we	us
you	you
they	them

We use object pronouns to replace an object in a sentence.
*He is opening **the book**.*
*He is opening **it**.*

*I see **my friend** every Saturday.*
*I see **him** every Saturday.*

3 **Complete the sentences and questions with object pronouns.**

1 She helps _____me_____ (I) with my homework.
2 I can't see _____ (the bus stop).
3 Can you read _____ (two books) in a week?
4 I can't hear _____ (my mother) in the kitchen.
5 She likes _____ (Tim).
6 Have you got _____ (the keys) in your bag?
7 They can't see _____ (we) from over there.
8 They don't want _____ (the cake).

4 **Find the mistakes in the sentences. Then write them correctly.**

1 Let's <u>eat not</u> now. Let's eat later.

   <u>Let's not eat now. Let's eat later.</u>

2 I saw he at the supermarket.

   _____

3 Don't you close the window.

   _____

4 Sit down and you open your books.

   _____

5 She likes they very much.

   _____

6 Let's to have a picnic tomorrow!

   _____

5 **Rewrite the sentences using the imperative.**

1 You mustn't eat all that cake.

   _____

2 You must finish your homework.

   _____

3 You mustn't go to bed very late.

   _____

4 You must cut the paper into three pieces.

   _____

5 You mustn't listen to her!

   _____

6 **Complete the sentences with *let's* or *let's not* and the verbs from the box.**

| call | ~~clean~~ | listen | play | watch |

1   <u>Let's not clean</u> our bedroom now. ✗

2 _____ tennis! ✔

3 _____ TV this evening. ✗

4 _____ to some music. ✔

5 _____ Mum. ✔

7 **Rewrite the sentences and questions using object pronouns.**

1 Please have <u>these flowers</u>.

   Please have them.

2 Let's call <u>Maria</u> now!

   _____

3 Can you see <u>the train</u>?

   _____

4 I'm waiting for <u>my parents</u>.

   _____

5 Do <u>your exercises</u> now, please.

   _____

6 <u>Freddie</u> wants to play with my brother and me.

   _____

8 **Complete the sentences with the verbs from the box.**

> be   eat   ~~forget~~   go (x2)   have (x2)
> invite   spend   ~~visit~~

1 **A:** Let's _____visit_____ our cousins later.

   B: OK, but don't _____forget_____ to buy them a present!

2 **A:** Let's _____ shopping today.

   B: OK, but don't _____ a lot of money.

3 **A:** Let's _____ a party this weekend.

   B: OK, but don't _____ lots of people!

4 **A:** Let's _____ pizza for dinner.

   B: OK, but don't _____ all of it!

5 **A:** Let's _____ for a walk by the sea!

   B: OK, but don't _____ late for lunch.

Pairwork

Work in pairs. Have short dialogues like the dialogues in Exercise 8.

Let's buy tickets for the cinema.

OK, but don't choose a scary film.

Writing

Think about the weekend. Write ten suggestions with *let's* and *let's not*.

Past simple: *to be*

Past simple: *to be*

Affirmative	Negative	Question
I was	I was not (wasn't)	Was I?
you were	you were not (weren't)	Were you?
he was	he was not (wasn't)	Was he?
she was	she was not (wasn't)	Was she?
it was	it was not (wasn't)	Was it?
we were	we were not (weren't)	Were we?
you were	you were not (weren't)	Were you?
they were	they were not (weren't)	Were they?

Short answers

Yes, I was.	No, I wasn't.	Yes, it was.	No, it wasn't.
Yes, you were.	No, you weren't.	Yes, we were.	No, we weren't.
Yes, he was.	No, he wasn't.	Yes, you were.	No, you weren't.
Yes, she was.	No, she wasn't.	Yes, they were.	No, they weren't.

The past simple of the verb *to be* is *was*/*were*.
*He **was** at work this morning.*   *We **were** at the beach yesterday.*

The negative is formed by putting the word *not* after the verb. The short form is *wasn't*/*weren't*.
*I **wasn't** at a football match last Saturday.*

The question is formed by changing the word order of the subject and the verb.
***Were you** awake all night?*

Notes

We use time expressions such as *yesterday, yesterday morning, last Saturday, last week*, etc. with the past simple. These expressions usually go at the beginning or the end of a sentence.

> My friend and I were
> here last week. It was
> an amazing holiday!

1 **Complete the sentences with *was* or *were*.**

1 They _____were_____ late for work this morning.

2 Johan _____ at a nice hotel last year.

3 My uncle _____ at home all weekend.

4 We _____ with some friends last Saturday.

5 You _____ quiet last night. What _____ the matter?

6 I _____ at the park yesterday.

7 Last summer, Mum and Dad _____ in Cyprus.

8 My cousin _____ at the swimming pool yesterday.

3 **Complete the questions with *was* or *were*. Then answer the questions.**

1 _____Were_____ you at home on Sunday evening? ✔

Yes, I was.

2 _____ Jim on holiday last August? ✔

_____

3 _____ your parents at the cinema on Saturday? ✗

_____

4 _____ the bag under the desk? ✔

_____

5 _____ the apples in the bag? ✔

_____

6 _____ she late for the lesson? ✗

_____

Think about it!

There is no affirmative short form for *to be* in the past simple.

2 **Make the sentences negative.**

1 My friend was at school today.

My friend wasn't at school today.

2 You were well yesterday.

_____

3 I was on the bus this afternoon.

_____

4 My cousin was at summer camp last month.

_____

5 We were very busy last spring.

_____

6 They were at work on Monday.

_____

7 The photos were on the table.

_____

8 The cake was in the fridge.

_____

4 **Write the words in the correct order.**

1 house / wasn't / the / yesterday / she / in

She wasn't in the house yesterday.

2 home / were / my dad / and I / all day / at

_____

3 was / Mum / garden / the / in

_____

4 park / boys / the / the / were / at / ?

_____

5 in / the / wasn't / teacher / classroom / the

_____

6 the / bed / comic book / on / was / the / ?

_____

7 children / last night / happy / the / weren't /

_____

8 the / good / was / weather / yesterday / ?

_____

5 **Write questions. Then write answers using the words in brackets.**

1 the boys / at school / last week / ?
(at home)

Were the boys at school last week?

No, they weren't. They were at home.

2 the explorer / on a plane / ? (on a boat)

_____

_____

3 Your sister / sad / yesterday / ? (happy)

_____

_____

4 Arya / at the cinema / last night / ?
(in the café)

_____

_____

5 the girls / in the house / yesterday / ?
(in the garden)

_____

_____

6 **Complete the text with *was, wasn't, were* or *weren't*.**

Last Saturday, I ¹ _____ was _____ at my friend Raul's house. His sister ² _____ there too, but his brother ³ _____ . The weather ⁴ _____ very good that day – it ⁵ _____ cold and wet.

Raul's room ⁶ _____ tidy at all! Lots of books ⁷ _____ on his desk and all his games ⁸ _____ on the floor! His mum and dad ⁹ _____ at home. They ¹⁰ _____ at his aunt's house.

At nine o'clock, it ¹¹ _____ time to go home. I ¹² _____ tired, but happy.

There was/there were

Affirmative	Negative	Question
there was	there was not (there wasn't)	Was there?
there were	there were not (there weren't)	Were there?

Short answers	
Yes, there was.	No, there wasn't.
Yes, there were.	No, there weren't.

We use *there was* and *there were* to talk or ask about what existed when we are describing something in the past.
There was a sailing boat on the sea.
There were lots of people at the party.

7 **Complete the sentences and questions with *there was* or *there were*.**

1 There weren't a lot of trees in the park. ✗
2 _____ a panda at the zoo?
3 _____ big fish in the river. ✔
4 _____ eggs in the cake?
5 _____ a salad in the fridge. ✔
6 _____ a boat on the sea. ✗
7 _____ people in the building. ✔
8 _____ blue flowers in the garden?

Pairwork

Work in pairs. Take turns to ask and answer the questions below.

- Where were you last summer?
- Were you at the beach?
- Were you in the mountains?
- Were you in a village?

- Was your best friend with you?
- Were you with your family?
- Were you happy there?
- Was the weather good?

Writing

Write a paragraph for the class magazine about last summer.

1 **Complete the sentences and questions with the present simple.**

1 They ___do not have___ (not have) badminton lessons on Saturdays.

2 She _____ (not like) milk.

3 _____ he _____ (speak) English?

4 They _____ (always / travel) by train.

5 We _____ (not like) very cold weather.

6 _____ you _____ (you / know) that person over there?

7 She _____ (run) very slowly.

8 _____ they _____ (live) in Spain?

2 **Complete the sentences and questions with the present continuous.**

1 She ___is playing___ (play) the piano at the moment.

2 Where is Mikael? _____ he _____ (visit) his friend?

3 The students _____ (study) hard this year.

4 I _____ (not do) my homework; I _____ (watch) a film.

5 _____ they _____ (learn) German this year?

6 She _____ (not have) dinner with us tonight.

7 The children _____ (make) toy planes.

8 We _____ (sit) in the park.

3 **Complete the sentences and questions with the present simple or continuous.**

1 They ___usually see___ (usually / see) their friends at the weekend.

2 Julia _____ (go) on holiday today.

3 George _____ (always / give) me a present on my birthday.

4 _____ they _____ (want) to go to the museum today?

5 It's late and they _____ (close) the shop now.

6 We _____ (never / work) on Saturdays.

7 _____ it _____ (rain) at the moment?

8 Listen! Your phone _____ (ring).

4 **Complete the sentences and questions with *can* and the verb in brackets.**

1   _____Can_____ I ____watch____ (watch) a film tonight?

2   You _____ (not leave) now! The film is starting.

3   _____ she _____ (borrow) your phone?

4   We _____ (not go) shopping now. Aunt Eva is here.

5   _____ you _____ (speak) Russian?

6   He _____ (not come) to the party next weekend.

7   They _____ (help) me cook dinner.

8   I _____ (not find) my watch.

5 **Write questions with *can*. Then answer the questions.**

1   we / have / juice with dinner / ? ✔
    Can we have juice with dinner?
    Yes, we can.

2   I / open the window / ? ✗
    _____
    _____

3   they / go to the cinema / ? ✔
    _____
    _____

4   he / come home with us / ? ✗
    _____
    _____

5   she / swim / ? ✔
    _____
    _____

6   he / do his maths homework / ? ✗
    _____
    _____

7   he / play the guitar / ? ✔
    _____
    _____

8   you / ride a horse / ? ✗
    _____
    _____

6 **Complete the sentences and questions with *must* and the verb in brackets.**

1   I _mustn't forget_ (not forget) my train ticket.

2   He _____ (do) his homework now.

3   We _____ (go) now. It's getting late.

4   _____ you _____ (clean) the house today?

5   She _____ (catch) the six o'clock bus to the station.

6   We _____ (not draw) on the desks.

7   They _____ (not talk) in the library.

8   _____ you _____ (make) that terrible noise?

7 **Match 1–8 with a–h. Then write sentences.**

1	Stand		a	your name.	1	_Stand up._
2	Open		b	up.	2	_____
3	Don't make		c	at page 34.	3	_____
4	Come		d	here.	4	_____
5	Look		e	quiet.	5	_____
6	Listen to		f	the window.	6	_____
7	Be		g	me.	7	_____
8	Write		h	a noise.	8	_____

8 **Write sentences with _let's_ or _let's not_.**

1 be / late / for school ✗

   Let's not be late for school. _____

2 buy / a game / for her birthday ✔

   _____

3 water / the plants ✔

   _____

4 watch / TV ✗

   _____

5 go / shopping ✗

   _____

6 have / breakfast ✔

   _____

7 call / our cousins ✔

   _____

8 tidy / our bedroom / today ✗

   _____

9 **Complete the sentences with object pronouns.**

1 Give _____ me _____ (I) the book, please.
2 I must visit _____ (he) tomorrow.
3 I don't want _____ (ice cream) now.
4 Can you see _____ (our friends)?
5 The artist is painting _____ (you and me) now.
6 Are you learning _____ (the new words)?
7 Can I meet _____ (your friend's sister)?
8 We all like _____ (your parents).

10 **Complete the sentences and questions with *there was* or *there were*.**

1 ___Was there___ a book on your desk?

2 _____ any cakes for the party. ✗

3 _____ some ducks on the lake. ✔

4 _____ three taxis outside the station. ✔

5 _____ any people swimming in the sea?

6 _____ any cars on the street. ✗

7 _____ a good programme on TV last night?

8 _____ a table in the middle of the room. ✔

11 **Complete the sentences with the past simple of *to be*.**

1 We ____were____ very tired last night. ✔

2 Dad _____ at work on Thursday. ✗

3 The pens _____ on the desk. ✔

4 He _____ at home at lunchtime. ✗

5 The eggs _____ in the fridge. ✔

6 We _____ on time for school yesterday. ✗

7 I _____ with my friends all day. ✔

8 They _____ at the sports centre last week. ✗

12 **Complete the questions with *was* or *were*. Then answer the questions.**

1 ____Were____ the tickets in the bag? ✔

Yes, they were.

2 _____ he late for the lesson? ✗

_____

3 _____ my parents at the meeting? ✗

_____

4 _____ you late for the bus? ✔

_____

5 _____ Gemma at home on Friday? ✗

_____

6 _____ you on holiday last July? ✔

_____

7 _____ the bag under the bed? ✗

_____

8 _____ your friends at the cinema on Sunday? ✔

_____

Past simple affirmative: regular and irregular verbs

> Yesterday, I cleaned my bedroom. I made my bed, tidied my desk and watered the plants. Today, I'm not doing anything!

Past simple affirmative

Regular verbs	Irregular verbs
I worked	I went
you worked	you went
he worked	he went
she worked	she went
it worked	it went
we worked	we went
you worked	you went
they worked	they went

We use the past simple to talk about:

- things in the past which have finished.
  *I **went** to work at eight o'clock.*

- things in the past which were habits.
  *Last year, he **cycled** to school every day.*

- things in the past which happened one after the other.
  *She **opened** the front door, **went** inside and **put** down her bag.*

We form the past simple affirmative of regular verbs by adding the *-ed* ending.
work → *work**ed***

When the verb ends in *-e*, we add *-d*.
bake → *bak**ed***

When the verb ends in a consonant and *-y*, we take off the *-y* and add *-ied*.
carry → *carr**ied***

When the verb ends in a vowel and -*y*, we just add -*ed*.

stay   →   *st**ayed***

When the verb ends in a vowel and a consonant and that vowel is stressed, we double the last consonant and add -*ed*.

permit   →   *perm**itted***

When the verb ends in -*l*, we double the -*l* and add -*ed*.

cancel   →   *cance**lled***

There are many irregular verbs in English. We do not form the past simple of these verbs by adding -*ed*. See the irregular verbs list on page 128.

1 **Complete the sentences with the past simple.**

1 They _____talked_____ (talk) all evening.

2 We _____ (walk) by the river in the morning.

3 Dad _____ (fix) my bike yesterday.

4 People _____ (smile) at the camera.

5 The chef _____ (cook) a tasty meal for us.

6 I _____ (want) to leave the party early.

7 She _____ (paint) a great picture of an elephant.

8 He _____ (listen) to his favourite music all morning.

> **Think about it!**
>
> We do not double the *n* in *listen* because we stress the first, not the second, syllable.

2 **Complete the table.**

Verb	Past simple
begin	began
break	
build	
come	
do	
drive	
fall	
find	
fly	
get	
know	
learn	
meet	
spend	
say	
think	

3 **Complete the sentences with the past simple.**

1 They _____took_____ (take) their grandmother to the station.

2 Mum _____ (make) a chocolate cake for my birthday.

3 We _____ (buy) our son a tablet last month.

4 The students _____ (sit) quietly in the classroom.

5 I _____ (write) a postcard to my cousin.

6 We _____ (do) our homework quickly after school.

7 She _____ (come) to Edu's party with Parina.

8 The man _____ (sing) loudly in the shower.

> *Ago*
>
> We use the word *ago* to talk about something that happened a number of years, minutes, days, etc. in the past.
>
> *I **bought** this house **two months ago**.*
> *He **arrived ten minutes ago**.*
> *Harry **went** to bed **three hours ago**.*

4 **Write sentences with *ago*.**

1   He went there in March. It is now October.
     He went there seven months ago.

2   She visited us in September. It is now August.
     _____

3   She was born in 2016.
     _____

4   She phoned us at eight o'clock. It is now nine o'clock.
     _____

5   We saw them this time last year.
     _____

6   I learnt to swim when I was seven. I am now twelve.
     _____

5 **Write the words in the correct order.**

1   the / last / cinema / went / to / we / night
     We went to the cinema last night.

2   visited / two / us / ago / she / years
     _____

3   last / I / email / a / long / wrote / night
     _____

4   my / flew / into / garden / birds / three
     _____

5   a / sandwich / hour / ate / she / an / ago
     _____

6   friend / met / beach / I / at / a / the
     _____

7   teacher / spoke / quietly / to the children / the
     _____

8   yesterday / the / Mr Davis / left / office / early
     _____

6 **Find the mistakes in the sentences. Then write them correctly.**

1   I <u>come</u> to this school three years ago.
     I came to this school three years ago.

2   They were had a nice time yesterday.
     _____

3   He teach us Spanish last year.
     _____

4   We go to the cinema four days ago.
     _____

5   He broke his leg ago a week.
     _____

Think about it!

We put the time phrase at the beginning or the end of the sentence. If we put it at the beginning, we use a comma after it.

Yesterday, *I went to a theme park.*

I went to a theme park *yesterday*.

7 **Complete the sentences with the past simple. Use the verbs from the box.**

| ask | deliver | ~~have~~ |
| open | start | walk |

1   I _____had_____ lunch at one o'clock.

2   He _____ home with his friends.

3   The children _____ their presents quickly.

4   The rain _____ in the morning.

5   The woman _____ some flowers.

6   The teacher _____ a question.

8 Complete the text with the past simple.

One day last summer, my parents
1 _____visited_____ (visit) an old
castle outside their town. The day
2 _____ (begin) very well
because it 3 _____ (be) hot and
sunny. My dad 4 _____ (take)
his camera with him and my mum
5 _____ (drive) them there
in her car. They 6 _____
(spend) all day at the castle and
they 7 _____ (learn) a
lot about its history. At lunchtime,
they 8 _____ (sit) on the
grass and 9 _____ (have)
a picnic. At the castle shop, Mum
10 _____ (buy) some
postcards and Dad
11 _____ (get) an ice cream.
It 12 _____ (be) a really nice
day out!

9 Complete the sentences with the past simple. Use the verbs from the box.

drive	fly	like	look	meet
~~play~~	see	shout	study	wash

1 The children _____played_____ in the park all day.

2 He _____ a balloon in the sky.

3 He _____ his car to work.

4 They _____ from Sydney to Bangkok last year.

5 We _____ our friends in town at lunchtime.

6 I _____ my face and went to bed.

7 We _____ the food at your party. It was tasty.

8 She _____ history at university.

9 She _____ in the mirror and smiled.

10 He _____ for help when he saw the accident.

Pairwork

Work in pairs. Talk about what you did last weekend.

On Saturday, I studied for my exams all morning. Then, I had lunch.

Writing

Write a postcard to a friend about a trip you went on. Include the points below.

- where you went
- who you went with
- how you went there

- what you saw
- what you ate
- what you did

Past simple negative and question

Welcome back! Did you have a good trip?

Yes, we did. It was amazing!

Past simple negative and question

Affirmative	Negative	Question
I worked	I did not (didn't) work	Did I work?
you worked	you did not (didn't) work	Did you work?
he worked	he did not (didn't) work	Did he work?
she worked	she did not (didn't) work	Did she work?
it worked	it did not (didn't) work	Did it work?
we worked	we did not (didn't) work	Did we work?
you worked	you did not (didn't) work	Did you work?
they worked	they did not (didn't) work	Did they work?

Short answers

Yes, I did.	No, I didn't.	Yes, it did.	No, it didn't.
Yes, you did.	No, you didn't.	Yes, we did.	No, we didn't.
Yes, he did.	No, he didn't.	Yes, you did.	No, you didn't.
Yes, she did.	No, she didn't.	Yes, they did.	No, they didn't.

The negative of the past simple (regular and irregular verbs) is formed with the auxiliary verb *did*, the word *not* and the infinitive (without *to*).
*The train **didn't arrive** on time.*

The question form of the past simple (regular and irregular verbs) is formed with *did* and the infinitive (without *to*).
***Did** the train **arrive** on time?*

1 Complete the sentences with the negative form of the past simple.

1 They ___didn't stay___ (stay) at the hotel because it was full.

2 The car _____ (stop) at the traffic lights.

3 Our friends _____ (arrive) early enough for lunch.

4 She _____ (clean) the windows yesterday.

5 My grandparents _____ (look) at all the photos.

6 Felipe _____ (play) football yesterday.

7 The children _____ (climb) trees in the park.

8 I _____ (walk) to work this morning.

2 Complete the questions with the past simple.

1 _Did they study_ (they / study) hard yesterday?

2 _____ (you / invite) all our friends to the party?

3 _____ (she / help) with the shopping?

4 _____ (the student / talk) to the teacher?

5 _____ (you / brush) your teeth this morning?

6 _____ (we / finish) all the food?

7 _____ (they / travel) by plane or by boat?

8 _____ (the boy / cry) when he hurt his foot?

3 Make the sentences negative.

1 Dad made a pizza yesterday.

  Dad didn't make a pizza yesterday.

2 I wrote an email to my uncle.

  _____

3 She broke all the glasses.

  _____

4 They came to work late yesterday.

  _____

5 He put away all his toys.

  _____

6 We met our friends at the funfair.

  _____

7 They built a house near the sea.

  _____

8 You gave me the keys.

  _____

Think about it!

Be careful with the verb *do*.

Affirmative: I **did** my homework.

Negative: I **didn't do** my homework.

Question: **Did** you **do** your homework?

4 **Write questions.**

1 The ball fell in the river.

  <u>Did the ball fall in the river?</u>

2 She found her phone.

  _____

3 They flew to India.

  _____

4 You thought about it carefully.

  _____

5 She made soup this afternoon.

  _____

6 You sang in the concert.

  _____

7 Our team won the match.

  _____

8 They left the meeting early.

  _____

5 **Write questions for the answers.**

1 <u>Did he go to the UK?</u>

  Yes, he went to the UK.

2 _____

  Yes, they had a nice time.

3 _____

  No, I didn't do any work.

4 _____

  Yes, she wrote a good story.

5 _____

  No, he didn't drive there.

6 _____

  Yes, they visited the waterfall.

7 _____

  Yes, he played tennis yesterday.

8 _____

  No, I didn't run around the park.

6 **Write the words in the correct order.**

1 didn't / he / you / see / there

     He didn't see you there.

2 do / homework / she / her / did / ?

     _____

3 speak / her / to / I / didn't

     _____

4 rain / didn't / it / yesterday

     _____

5 door / lock / didn't / you / the

     _____

6 you / car / did / wash / the / ?

     _____

Pairwork

Work in pairs. Take turns to ask and answer the questions below about last weekend.

- Did you wake up early on Saturday morning?
- Did you have a big breakfast?
- Did you go shopping?
- Did you stay at home on Saturday afternoon?
- Did you enjoy yourself on Saturday evening?

- Did you see your friends?
- Did you wake up early on Sunday morning?
- Did you do anything interesting on Sunday?
- Did you spend the day with your family?
- Did you go to bed early on Sunday?

Writing

Write ten things you didn't do when you were on holiday, but that you wanted to do.

Some, any, no

We use the word *some* before a noun in an affirmative sentence to say that something exists.
There's **some** juice in the fridge.
There are **some** magazines in my room.

We use the word *any* in negative sentences and questions to say that something doesn't exist or to ask if something exists.
He hasn't got **any** maths lessons today.
Are there **any** eggs in the fridge?

We use the word *no* with an affirmative verb to make a sentence negative in meaning.
There are **no** people on the train.
(There **aren't any** people on the train.)

Notes

We can use the word *some* in questions when we are asking for something or offering something.
Can I have **some** new boots, please?
Can I get you **some** more juice?

1 **Complete the sentences and questions with *some* or *any*.**

1 The farmers need _____some_____ rain. It's very hot and dry.

2 There aren't _____ crisps on the table.

3 Have you got _____ money?

4 Can I have _____ water, please?

5 We haven't got _____ noodles to make noodle soup.

6 I can see _____ children in the street.

7 We haven't got _____ pets.

8 Are there _____ shops near your home?

Look! I can see something over there.

Really? I can't see anything.

2 **Complete the sentences and questions with *any* or *no*.**

1 I haven't got _____ any _____ money in my purse.

2 Did you buy _____ tickets for the cinema?

3 There was _____ rain all summer.

4 There is _____ honey in the jar.

5 There wasn't _____ noise in the classroom.

6 He hasn't got _____ homework tonight.

7 There are _____ taxis today.

8 She can't find _____ fruit in the fridge.

Someone, anyone, no one, everyone

People	Things	Places
someone/somebody	something	somewhere
anyone/anybody	anything	anywhere
no one/nobody	nothing	nowhere
everyone/everybody	everything	everywhere

We usually use the words that begin with *some-* in affirmative sentences.

We use the words *someone* and *somebody* to talk about one unspecified person. There is no difference between *someone* and *somebody*.
***Someone** called you this morning.*

We use the word *something* to talk about one unspecified thing.
*There's **something** in my shoe.*

We use the word *somewhere* to talk about one unspecified place.
*I left my sunglasses **somewhere**!*

We use the words *anyone/anybody*, *anything* and *anywhere* to talk about one unspecified person, thing or place. We usually use the words that begin with *any-* in negative sentences and questions.
*There wasn't **anybody** at home.*
*Is there **anyone** here?*
*I can't find **anything** to wear for the party.*

We use the words *no one/nobody*, *nothing* and *nowhere* in affirmative sentences when the verb is affirmative but the meaning of the sentence is negative.
***No one** heard him.*
*I ate **nothing** all morning.*
*There is **nowhere** for me to sit.*

We use the words *everyone/everybody*, *everything* and *everywhere* to talk about all the people, things or places.

When the words *everyone/everybody* and *everything* are the subjects of a sentence, they are followed by a verb in the third person singular.
Everyone *was at the party.*
I paid for ***everything***.
He looked ***everywhere*** *for his glasses.*

3 **Complete the sentences and questions with *someone*, *anyone* or *everyone*.**

1 They asked ___everyone___ to the party. The whole street came!

2 I can't see _____ outside. It's very dark!

3 Can _____ help me, please?

4 There wasn't _____ at school when I got there.

5 _____ in the class got good marks in the exam.

6 What's that noise? Is _____ shouting in the street?

4 **Rewrite the sentences using the word in bold.**
   Use between two and five words.

1 There isn't anyone on the bus. **no one**
   There _____is no one_____ on the bus.

2 There is nothing I can do about your problem. **anything**
   There _____ I can do about your problem.

3 There isn't anywhere we can hide. **nowhere**
   There _____ we can hide.

4 There was nothing good on TV last night. **anything**
   There _____ good on TV last night.

5 There wasn't anybody in the room. **nobody**
   There _____ in the room.

6 There is no information about the subject on the internet. **any**
   There _____ about the subject on the internet.

Think about it!

We can use *some* and words with *some* in questions to offer something to someone or to ask for something.

Think about it!

We cannot use *everyone* or *everybody* after *there is*.

5 **Circle the correct answer.**

1   I can't find my bag. It isn't ___ in the house.

   a   nowhere   b   anywhere   c   somewhere

2   I like ___ in that clothes shop!

   a   anything   b   everywhere   c   everything

3   I know my keys are ___ in the house!

   a   somewhere   b   anywhere   c   everywhere

4   Did you see ___ on the floor?

   a   nothing   b   everywhere   c   anything

5   There is ___ in the garden.

   a   somebody   b   anybody   c   everybody

6   We went ___ last weekend.

   a   anywhere   b   nowhere   c   anybody

Pairwork

Work in pairs. Make up an adventure story using the words from this unit.

Writing

Write an adventure story. Use the words from this unit.

UNIT 16

Countable and uncountable nouns and quantifiers

Countable and uncountable nouns

Countable nouns		Uncountable nouns	
bottle	pencil	bread	milk
chair	programme	cheese	money
computer	sandwich	food	pasta
invitation	tablet	furniture	tea
notebook	woman	meat	water

Nouns that we can count and that we can use in the plural are called countable nouns. When the subject of a sentence is in the plural, the verb must also be in the plural.

There **are** three **factories** in the city.

They have got five **children**.

Nouns that we cannot count and that do not have plurals are called uncountable nouns. We do not use *a* and *an* with uncountable nouns. When the subject of a sentence is an uncountable noun, the verb must be in the singular.

The **food was** delicious.

The **bread is** fresh.

We can use other words with uncountable nouns so that we know how much we have, such as *a bottle of* (*water*), *a slice of* (*bread*), *a piece of* (*cheese*), *a glass of* (*milk*), *a kilo of* (*butter*), *a plate of* (*pasta*), etc.

How many people can we invite to the party?

And how much food do we need?

We can use the word *some* in front of countable and uncountable nouns in affirmative sentences.
*There are **some** eggs in the box.*   *There is **some** water in the bottle.*

We can use the word *any* in front of countable and uncountable nouns in negative sentences and questions.
*There aren't **any** dogs in the park.*   *Is there **any** milk left?*

We can use the word *no* in front of countable and uncountable nouns with an affirmative verb to give a sentence a negative meaning.
*There are **no** books on the shelf.*   *There is **no** medicine in the bathroom.*

1 **Complete the sentences with *a, an* or *some*.**

1   There's _____a_____ big blue bowl on the kitchen table.

2   There are _____ fresh vegetables in the fridge.

3   I want to buy _____ red apples from the supermarket.

4   The teacher's got _____ old coat in his cupboard.

5   I must get _____ food for your dinner tonight!

6   You made _____ small mistake in this exercise.

7   We met _____ interesting people at the beach.

8   She wants to be _____ actor.

2 **Circle the correct the answer.**

1   (Is)/ *Are* there any juice in the fridge?

2   The milk *is / are* not fresh. We must get some more.

3   There *is / are* six hundred people in this building.

4   This soup *is / are* awful! I can't eat it.

5   There *isn't / aren't* any clothes on the bed.

6   The food in this restaurant *is / are* really excellent!

7   *Is / Are* the cheese from France?

8   The strawberries *is / are* very sweet and juicy.

Think about it!

We do not use *a* or *an* with uncountable nouns.

3   **Match 1–8 with a–h to make phrases. Then write the phrases under the pictures.**

1	a loaf of	a	rice	
2	a carton of	b	coffee	
3	a jar of	c	chocolate	
4	a packet of	d	honey	
5	a bottle of	e	bread	
6	a cup of	f	cheese	
7	a bar of	g	water	
8	a piece of	h	milk	

1   <u>a loaf of bread</u>   2 _____   3 _____   4 _____

5 _____   6 _____   7 _____   8 _____

Much and *many*

We use *much* with uncountable nouns in negative sentences and questions.
*He doesn't earn **much** money.*
*Have you got **much** work this week?*

We use the word *many* with countable nouns in negative sentences and questions.
*There aren't **many** people in the shop.*
*Have you got **many** books about horses?*

When we ask about quantity, we use *how much …?* for uncountable nouns and *how many …?* for countable nouns.
*How **much** bread is there?*
*How **many** children were at the party?*

4   **Complete the sentences and questions with *much* or *many*.**

1   We don't have _____ much _____ money left.

2   Are there _____ dangerous snakes in Africa?

3   He doesn't have _____ furniture in his new house.

4   There isn't _____ soup left for me!

5   Has he got _____ friends at school?

6   There aren't _____ flowers in the garden.

7   Were there _____ loaves of bread on the shelf?

8   There isn't _____ meat on his pizza.

5 **Complete the questions with *much* or *many*.**

1 How _____ much _____ cheese do you want?

2 How _____ plates are there in the cupboard?

3 How _____ video games have they got?

4 How _____ water is there in the bottle?

5 How _____ books did you borrow?

6 How _____ sugar did you put in the cake?

7 How _____ mistakes did you make?

8 How _____ meat do you eat every week?

A little, a few, a lot/lots of

We use *a little* with uncountable nouns when we want to say that a small amount of something exists. It has a positive meaning.
A: *Can I have something to eat?*
B: *Yes, there's **a little** bread and some cheese on the table.*

We use *a few* with countable nouns when we want to say that a small number of something exists. It has a positive meaning.
*There are **a few** tickets left for the football match.*

We use *a lot* (*of*) and *lots* (*of*) with countable nouns and uncountable nouns in affirmative and negative sentences, and in questions.
*We have got **a lot of** cousins.*
*There are **lots of** hotels in Spain.*
*Has he got **lots of** friends?*
*They haven't got **a lot of** money.*

---

6 **Complete the sentences and questions with *a few* or *a little*.**

1 She made _____ a few _____ mistakes in the test.

2 There is _____ orange juice in the fridge.

3 Can I have _____ water, please?

4 They saw _____ good films last year.

5 I've got _____ money in my bag.

6 Belen wants _____ new clothes for her holiday.

7 We met _____ interesting people at the party.

8 The pasta needs _____ cheese.

7 **Circle the correct answer.**

1   She's got ___ cousins.

   a   much   **b**   a few   c   a little

2   How ___ food is in the fridge?
Do we need to buy any?

   a   many   b   much   c   a little

3   He hasn't got ___ friends.

   a   many   b   much   c   lots

4   You've got ___ games!

   a   much   b   lots of   c   a little

5   I want ___ cheese on my spaghetti.

   a   much   b   a little   c   many

6   We bought ___ nice books from the shop.

   a   a little   b   lots   c   a few

7   Are there ___ interesting places near your house?

   a   many   b   much   c   a little

8   Is there ___ milk in the carton?

   a   many   b   lots   c   much

8 **Complete the text with the words from the box.**

a (x2)   any   ~~few~~   lots   piece (x2)   much   some (x2)

Last Saturday, Vicky and her friends went to a restaurant because it was her birthday. They went early and there were only a ¹ _____few_____ people there. Vicky didn't want ² _____ food because she was too excited about her birthday. But her friend was very hungry! He ordered a large ³ _____ of meat, ⁴ _____ of chips and ⁵ _____ bowl of salad. Vicky's other friend ordered ⁶ _____ fish. Vicky didn't want ⁷ _____ meat or fish, so she ordered ⁸ _____ green salad. They all drank ⁹ _____ juice. Then, they all wished her a very happy birthday with a ¹⁰ _____ of cake!

9 **Complete the sentences and questions with the words from the box.**

> any   few   how   little   lot   lots   ~~much~~   some

1 How _____much_____ milk do you want?
2 He's got _____ chocolate in his bag.
3 They haven't got _____ books to read.
4 I've got a _____ of things to do today.
5 There are only a _____ bananas in the bowl.
6 _____ much ice cream do we need?
7 She wants a _____ sauce on her pasta.
8 They did _____ of interesting things on holiday.

Pairwork

Work in pairs. Take turns to ask and answer about what you have got and what you haven't got. Use the ideas below.

- clothes
- bags
- books
- games
- friends
- money
- brothers/sisters
- pets

> Have you got lots of clothes?

> No, I haven't. I've got a few pairs of jeans and some T-shirts.

> Have you got lots of shoes?

> I haven't got any shoes, but I've got a lot of trainers.

Writing

Write a short paragraph about what you have got and what you haven't got. Use the words from this unit.

1 **Complete the sentences with the past simple.**

1   His dad ____prepared____ (prepare) a special meal for his birthday.
2   I _____ (try) to make spaghetti, but it wasn't very good!
3   The artist _____ (paint) pictures of the countryside.
4   The young man _____ (carry) my heavy shopping for me.
5   They _____ (talk) on the phone all evening.
6   We _____ (walk) through the old part of the village.
7   I _____ (clean) the house yesterday.
8   They _____ (travel) over the mountains on a sled.

2 **Complete the table.**

Verbs	Past simple
break	broke
catch	
draw	
drink	
eat	
fall	
get	
have	
know	
learn	
make	
sit	
speak	
spend	
take	
think	

3 **Complete the sentences with the past simple.**

1   I _____came_____ (come) home early last night.
2   We _____ (do) our homework very quickly yesterday.
3   I _____ (lose) my keys yesterday.
4   They _____ (drive) their friends to the airport.
5   I _____ (feel) ill, so I stayed at home.
6   Ben _____ (buy) a new bike last month.
7   The students _____ (write) down everything the teacher said.
8   She _____ (send) an email to her friend this morning.

4 **Complete the sentences with the negative form of the past simple.**

1 We ___didn't look___ (look) at all the photos.
2 He _____ (walk) to the shops this morning.
3 We _____ (make) a lot of mistakes in our homework.
4 My cousin _____ (play) basketball yesterday.
5 I _____ (watch) TV last night.
6 The chef _____ (break) a plate at lunchtime.
7 We _____ (learn) all the words on the test this morning.
8 My brother _____ (fly) to Hawaii last January.

5 **Complete the questions with the past simple.**

1 _____Did they drive_____ (they / drive) to Poland?
2 _____ (Deka / cry) when she fell over?
3 _____ (you / know) about her new job?
4 _____ (the ball / fall) out of the window?
5 _____ (we / finish) all the pizza?
6 _____ (you / brush) your hair this morning?
7 _____ (you / find) your ticket?
8 _____ (they / travel) to Peru?

6 **Write sentences and questions with the past simple.**

1 he / buy flowers / for his mother / ?
   Did he buy flowers for his mother?

2 I / not spend time / with my friends
   _____

3 you / walk to school / yesterday / ?
   _____

4 they / fly to Mumbai / last night / ?
   _____

5 she / not go to summer camp / last year
   _____

6 it / rain in Spain / last week / ?
   _____

7 we / not watch TV / last night
   _____

8 you / speak to David / last weekend / ?
   _____

7 **Complete the sentences and questions with *some* or *any*.**

1 I can see _____some_____ birds in the trees.

2 We don't have _____ bread.

3 Are there _____ parks where you live?

4 We don't need _____ help, thanks.

5 We want _____ good weather this weekend.

6 There aren't _____ glasses on the table.

7 Have you got _____ money?

8 Here are _____ presents for you.

8 **Complete the sentences and questions with *any* or *no*.**

1 He doesn't need to do _____any_____ work this evening.

2 There are _____ buses today.

3 He can't find _____ pencils.

4 There are _____ bowls on the table.

5 I haven't got _____ bread.

6 Did you buy _____ clothes for the trip?

7 There wasn't _____ snow all winter.

8 There is _____ milk in the carton.

9 **Complete the sentences and questions with *someone*, *anyone* or *everyone*.**

1 _____Everyone_____ in the class went to the wildlife park.

2 I need _____ to help me. Ivan, can you help?

3 There's _____ at the door. Can you open it, please?

4 When the bell rang, _____ went home.

5 Hello? Is there _____ there?

6 Can _____ do the washing up, please?

7 _____ was happy when they heard the good news.

8 I didn't know _____ at first, but I soon made friends.

10 **Circle the correct answer.**

1 There were ___ people at the party.

  a much   b any   c a lot of

2 Is there ___ ice cream in the freezer?

  a many   b a lot   c much

3 How ___ pairs of jeans has he got?

  a many   b any   c much

4 We haven't got ___ cheese.

  a many   b much   c a few

5 He's got ___ good friends.

  a any   b a few   c lots

6 There are ___ exercises in this book.

  a much   b a little   c a lot of

7 He hasn't got ___ money.

  a many   b much   c some

8 Are there ___ interesting old buildings in your town?

  a any   b much   c a little

11 **Complete the table with the words from the box.**

| book | bread | egg | fork | honey | knife | milk | money | orange |
| potato | rice | sandwich | spaghetti | sugar | vegetable | water |

Countable nouns	Uncountable nouns
book	

12 **Match 1–8 with a–h.**

1 a carton of   a honey

2 a loaf of   b bread

3 a packet of   c cake

4 a bottle of   d chocolate

5 a cup of   e milk

6 a bar of   f rice

7 a jar of   g water

8 a piece of   h coffee

UNIT 17

Comparative and superlative

> We're faster. We're stronger. We're fitter. We're the best!

Comparative

We use the comparative form to compare two people, animals or things. We often use the word *than* after the comparative form.

*He's **taller than** me.*
*The toy dinosaur is **more expensive than** the toy bear.*

To make the comparative form of adjectives with one syllable, we add the ending *-er*.

tall   →   tall**er**

When the adjective ends in *-e*, we just add *-r*.

late   →   late**r**

When the adjective ends in a vowel and a consonant, we double the last consonant and add *-er*.

fat   →   fa**tter**

When an adjective ends in *-y*, we take off the *-y* and add *-ier*.

early   →   earl**ier**

Sometimes we use the word *more* with two-syllable adjectives to make the comparative form.

famous   →   **more famous**

Some two-syllable adjectives have two comparative forms.

simple   →   simpl**er**/**more simple**
clever   →   clever**er**/**more clever**
polite   →   polit**er**/**more polite**

We use the word *more* to make the comparative form of adjectives with three or more syllables.

confusing   →   **more confusing**

Some adjectives are irregular and do not follow these rules.

good   →   **better**
bad   →   **worse**

1 **Complete the sentences with the comparative form.**

1   The ship is _____bigger_____ (big) than the boat.

2   Their children are _____ (polite) than other children.

3   The flowers _____ (beautiful) than the plants.

4   The football fans were _____ (noisy) than the tennis fans.

5   Spain is _____ (warm) than the UK.

6   The baby's teddy bear is _____ (fat) than hers.

7   A motorbike is _____ (dangerous) than a car.

8   This bag is _____ (heavy) than that one.

Think about it!

We do not use *more* with adjective + *-er*
I'm ~~more~~ shorter than my brother.

Superlative

We use the superlative form to compare more than two people, animals or things. We often use a phrase beginning with *in* or *of* to continue the sentence.
*She's **the most intelligent** girl **in** the school!*
*She's **the tallest of** all her sisters.*

To make the superlative form of adjectives with one syllable, we add the ending *-est*. We use the word *the* before the adjective in its superlative form.
tall   →   **the tallest**

When the adjective ends in *-e*, we just add *-st*.
late   →   **the latest**

When the adjective ends in a vowel and a consonant, we double the last consonant and add *-est*.
fit   →   **the fittest**

When an adjective ends in *-y*, we take off the *-y* and add *-iest*.
happy   →   the happ**iest**

Sometimes we use *the most* with a two-syllable adjective to make the superlative form.
famous → **the most famous**

Some two-syllable adjectives have two superlative forms.
simple   →   **the simplest/the most simple**
clever   →   **the cleverest/the most clever**
polite   →   **the politest/the most polite**

We use the word *most* to make the superlative form of adjectives with three or more syllables.
confusing →   **the most confusing**

Some adjectives are irregular and do not follow these rules.
good   →   **the best**
bad   →   **the worst**

Notes

The words *much*, *many*, *a lot/lots* (*of*), *a little* and *a few* also have comparative and superlative forms.

much	→	*more*	→	**the most**
many	→	*more*	→	**the most**
a lot (*of*)	→	*more*	→	**the most**
lots (*of*)	→	*more*	→	**the most**
a little	→	*less*	→	**the least**
a few	→	*fewer*	→	**the fewest**

2 **Complete the sentences with the superlative form.**

1 She is ___the nicest___ (nice) person I know.

2 Tuesday is _____ (bad) day of the week for me.

3 Her project was _____ (interesting) one in the class.

4 At our restaurant you can eat _____ (tasty) food in town!

5 Those exercises are _____ (difficult) of all.

6 She's _____ (old) daughter in the family.

7 Today is _____ (hot) day of the year.

8 _____ (exciting) ride at the funfair is the roller coaster.

As ... as

We can also use (*not*) *as ... as* to compare two people, animals or things.

We use *as ... as* when the two people, animals or things are the same.
*He is **as tall as** his father.*

We use *not as ... as* when they are different.
*This book is**n't as good as** that book.*

---

3 **Rewrite the sentences using *as ... as* or *not as ... as* and the word in bold.**

1 This mountain is 902 metres. That mountain is 902 metres. **high**

This mountain is
_____as high as_____ that mountain.

2 Aunt Bella is 45 years old. Aunt Serena is 44 years old. **young**

Aunt Bella is _____
Aunt Serena.

3 The elephant weighs 3,000 kilograms. The giraffe weighs 1,200 kilograms. **heavy**

The giraffe is _____
the elephant.

4 The house has got three bedrooms. The flat has got two bedrooms. **big**

The flat is _____
the house.

5 David scored nine points in the competition. Nancy scored nine points in the competition. **good**

Nancy's score was
_____ David's.

6 Nikos can lift 48 kilograms. Yuri can lift 55 kilograms. **strong**

Nikos is _____ Yuri.

4 **Write the words in the correct order.**

1 at tennis / Tony / than / brother / his / is / better
Tony is better than his brother
at tennis.

2 more / learning / important / than / is / studying
_____
_____

3 the / is / player / the / she / best / team / in
_____
_____

4 is / this / as / ours / as / flat / big
_____
_____

5 exercise / than / is / the / easier / others / this
_____
_____

6 in / popular / she / the US / the / actor / is / most
_____
_____

5 **Complete the sentences with one word in each gap.**

1 She's more interested in science
_____than_____ her sister.

2 The maths questions aren't
_____ difficult as you think.

3 This is _____ best day of my life!

4 *The Lord of the Rings* is the
_____ exciting book in the world!

5 He is _____ as friendly as his brother.

6 He's the most famous film star _____ the world.

6 **Complete the text with the comparative or superlative form.**

There's a boy in my town called Tomas. He's
1 _____older_____ (old) than I am, but he goes to the same school. His house is
2 _____ (big) than ours, but his garden is 3 _____ (small).

Tomas is 4 _____ (clever) boy in school and he's also 5 _____ (funny)! He loves jokes and he makes everyone laugh. His mum makes
6 _____ (good) cakes and Tomas is
7 _____ (hungry) than anybody else at break time. He eats a lot of cake!

Tomas is 8 _____ (good) than me at swimming, but I run 9 _____ (fast) than he does. Tomas has got lots of friends because he's very friendly. He's 10 _____ (popular) boy in town.

Pairwork

Work in pairs. Look at the three photos of holiday places and compare them with your partner. Use the words below.

- beautiful
- boring
- cheap
- cold
- exciting
- expensive
- few
- hot
- many
- ugly

Writing

Find three pictures of different places, people or animals and compare them. Write a short paragraph.

Be going to and future simple

Be going to

Affirmative	Negative	Question
I am (I'm) going to play	I am not (I'm not) going to play	Am I going to play?
you are (you're) going to play	you are not (you aren't) going to play	Are you going to play?
he is (he's) going to play	he is not (he isn't) going to play	Is he going to play?
she is (she's) going to play	she is not (she isn't) going to play	Is she going to play?
it is (it's) going to play	it is not (it isn't) going to play	Is it going to play?
we are (we're) going to play	we are not (we aren't) going to play	Are we going to play?
you are (you're) going to play	you are not (you aren't) going to play	Are you going to play?
they are (they're) going to play	they are not (they aren't) going to play	Are they going to play?

Short answers

Yes, I am.	No, I'm not.	Yes, it is.	No, it isn't.
Yes, you are.	No, you aren't.	Yes, we are.	No, we aren't.
Yes, he is.	No, he isn't.	Yes, you are.	No, you aren't.
Yes, she is.	No, she isn't.	Yes, they are.	No, they aren't.

Today, we're going to walk along this river.

It'll be an adventure!

We use *be going to* to talk about:

- future plans and arrangements.
  *Tomorrow, they **are going to** visit an art gallery.*

- something we know is going to happen because we have evidence.
  *Watch out! That glass **is going to** fall off the table!*

We can use time expressions such *as soon as, tomorrow, next week, this evening, in the morning, tonight, at the weekend, later on,* etc. with *be going to*.
*We **are going to** take the children to the circus **at the weekend**.*

1 **Complete the sentences and questions with *be going to* and the verb in brackets.**

1 I _____am going to have_____ (have) a shower tonight.

2 My cousins _____ (not visit) us this summer.

3 We _____ (not stay) out late this evening.

4 Look at those black clouds! It _____ (rain)!

5 I _____ (not write) those emails now.

6 He _____ (call) his friend later.

7 _____ the teacher _____ (give) us our test papers?

8 I _____ (not tell) him anything.

2 **Complete the questions with *be going to*. Then answer the questions.**

1 _____Are you going to watch_____
(you / watch) the film later? ✔
_Yes, I am._____

2 _____
(they / travel) by boat? ✔
_____

3 _____
(you / eat) all those cakes? ✘
_____

4 _____
(she / study) in the summer? ✔
_____

5 _____
(we / walk) home? ✔
_____

6 _____
(she / play) the piano later? ✘
_____

Think about it!

Don't forget to use *to* after *going*.

Future simple

Affirmative	Negative	Question
I will (I'll) play	I will not (won't) play	Will I play?
you will (you'll) play	you will not (won't) play	Will you play?
he will (he'll) play	he will not (won't) play	Will he play?
she will (she'll) play	she will not (won't) play	Will she play?
it will (it'll) play	it will not (won't) play	Will it play?
we will (we'll) play	we will not (won't) play	Will we play?
you will (you'll) play	you will not (won't) play	Will you play?
they will (they'll) play	they will not (won't) play	Will they play?

Short answers			
Yes, I will.	No, I won't.	Yes, it will.	No, it won't.
Yes, you will.	No, you won't.	Yes, we will.	No, we won't.
Yes, he will.	No, he won't.	Yes, you will.	No, you won't.
Yes, she will.	No, she won't.	Yes, they will.	No, they won't.

We use the future simple:

- for predictions for the future.
  *You **will** have two children and a long, happy life.*
- for decisions made at the time of speaking or to offer help.
  I'll carry that bag for you.
- for promises, threats and warnings.
  Stop climbing trees! You'll fall.
  *I **won't** be late. I promise.*

- to ask someone to do something for us.
  ***Will** you look after the children this weekend?*
- after *I hope, I think, I'm sure, I bet*, etc.
  ***I hope** you'll come and see us soon.*

We can use time expressions such *as soon as, tomorrow, next week, this evening, in the morning, tonight, at the weekend, later on,* etc. with the future simple.
*We **will** win the competition **at the weekend**.*

3 **Complete the questions with the future simple. Then answer the questions.**

1 _____Will he be_____ (he / be) at home this evening? ✗
  _No, he won't._____

2 _____ (you / help) me with these bags? ✔
  _____

3 _____ (she / be) fifteen next year? ✗
  _____

4 _____ (it / rain) later? ✔
  _____

5 _____ (they / have) dinner with us tomorrow? ✔
  _____

6 _____ (your dad / be) angry about the broken window? ✗
  _____

7 _____ (she / feel) better tomorrow, Doctor? ✔
  _____

8 _____ (you / make) breakfast for us this morning? ✗
  _____

4 **Complete the sentences with the future simple.**

1   I bet he ___won't have___ (not have) the same job next year.

2   We _____ (help) you with the shopping today.

3   She _____ (not know) her exam grades until next week.

4   They _____ (not invite) him to the party.

5   I know my friends _____ (tell) me.

6   I _____ (meet) you at nine o'clock in the morning.

7   The weather _____ (be) fine and sunny tomorrow.

8   Mina _____ (not buy) all the food we need.

5 **Complete the text with *be going to* or the future simple.**

It is two days before Olga and Akil's party ...

Olga: This afternoon, I [1] _____am going to buy_____ (buy) some things from the
supermarket, Akil. What [2] _____ (you / do)?

Akil: Well, I [3] _____ (get) the cake from the cake shop and then
I think I [4] _____ (check) who is coming to the party. I'm sure we
[5] _____ (have) a great time on Saturday, Olga!

Olga: [6] _____ (Cleo / come) to the party, Akil?

Akil: Yes, she is, so be careful! I hope you [7] _____ (not drop) cake over
her again!

Olga: No, don't worry. I promise I [8] _____ (not do) anything silly!

Pairwork

**Work in pairs. Take turns to ask and answer about your plans for the
summer holiday. Use the questions below.**

- Where are you going to go?
- Who is going to come with you?
- How are you going to travel there?
- What are you going to do?

Writing

**Write a short article for the school magazine about a place you are
going to visit in the summer. Say what you are going to do there.**

Question words

Question words

We use question words when we want more information than *yes* or *no*.
A: *Did you enjoy the film?*
B: *Yes, I did.*
A: *Why did you enjoy it?*
B: *Because it was a great adventure story and my favourite actor was in it.*

- *How*
We use *how* to ask about the way someone does something or to ask about someone's health.
How did he learn all those words?
How are you?

We can use *how* with adjectives and adverbs.
How old are they?
How often did you see them last year?
How many T-shirts have you got?
How much sugar did you put in the cake?

- *Who*
We use *who* to ask about people.
Who are they inviting to their party?

- *What*
We use *what* to ask about things or actions.
What happened?

- *When*
We use *when* to ask about time.
When do you want to leave?

- *Where*
We use *where* to ask about place.
Where did you put my bag?

- *Which*
We use *which* to ask about one person or thing within a group of similar people or things.
Which girl told you the news?

- *Whose*
We use *whose* to ask who something belongs to.
Whose bike will you ride?

- *Why*
We use *why* to ask about the reason for something.
Why are you crying?

What does the experiment show?

How long will the experiment take?

1 Tick (✔) the correct question, a or b.

1 a Where did he eat? ✔
  b Where he ate?

2 a Why you are reading?
  b Why are you reading?

3 a What his name was?
  b What was his name?

4 a What I can do?
  b What can I do?

5 a What your address is?
  b What is your address?

6 a When does the lesson begin?
  b When the lesson begins?

2 Complete the questions with *how, how much, how many, how old* or *how often*.

1 ___How often___ does he play basketball?
  Twice a week.

2 _____ do these jeans cost?
  25 euros.

3 _____ did you do in the test?
  Very well.

4 _____ children have they got?
  Two.

5 _____ are you?
  I'm fine.

6 _____ is your sister?
  She's ten.

Think about it!

We use *how much* in questions like *How much money have you got?* and *How much water have you got?*

Subject/object questions

Subject questions	Object questions
When the question word asks about the subject (the person, animal or thing that does the verb), then the verb stays in the affirmative form. **Who came** to the party? (*Lots of people came to the party.*) **Whose** grandparents **are** the oldest? (*My grandparents are the oldest.*)	When the question word asks about the object, then the verb changes to the question form. **What did** you buy? (*I bought a new game.*) **Which** book **do** you like? (*I like The Hobbit.*)

Notes

Do not confuse *whose?, who's?* (*who is?*) and *who's got?* (*who has got?*).
Whose guitar did you buy? (*I bought George's guitar.*)
Who's that woman over there? (*She's my mum's friend.*)
Who's got a brother? (*I've got a brother.*)

3 Circle the correct answer.

1 Who (*do you want*) / *you want* to see?
2 Who *does like* / *likes* ice cream?
3 Who *opened* / *did open* the door?

4 Who *is he having* / *is having* a party?
5 Who *you are* / *are you*?
6 Who *did run* / *ran* very fast in the race?

4 **Complete the questions with *whose* or *who's*.**

1 _____Who's_____ got a black pen?

2 _____ at the door?

3 _____ phone is ringing?

4 _____ shoes are in the kitchen?

5 _____ got an older sister or brother?

6 _____ the most popular actor in your country?

5 **Complete the questions with the words from the box.**

~~how~~   what   when   where   which   who   whose   why

1 _____How_____ old is your son?

2 _____ boots are you going to buy?

3 _____ tablet is this?

4 _____ are you opening the window?

5 _____ is he going to do?

6 _____ are we going home?

7 _____ are you at the moment?

8 _____ is that man next to your dad?

6 **Circle the correct answer.**

1 Which story (do you like)/ you like best?

2 Which student *did finish / finished* the exam first?

3 Which programme *did you watch / you watch* last weekend?

4 Which machine *does work / works* well?

5 Which camera *does take / takes* better photos?

6 Which pizza *did you order / you ordered*?

7 **Match the questions (1–10) with the answers (a–j).**

1 How old is your best friend?   a   By boat.

2 When did they arrive?   b   Last night.

3 How did you get to the island?   c   Not much.

4 Why are they so sad?   d   Three.

5 How many sisters have you got?   e   They're my cousins.

6 Who are those teenagers over there? f   She's eighteen.

7 What time do you usually get up?   g   At seven o'clock.

8 How much water is there in the bottle? h   Because their daughter is ill.

9 Whose bag is under the table?   i   The black one.

10 Which T-shirt do you like?   j   Rita's.

8 **Write questions. The underlined words are the answers.**

1 <u>Lara</u> invited Nihal to the party.

 Who invited Nihal to the party?

2 Lara invited <u>Nihal</u> to the party.

 _____

3 We go <u>to Italy</u> every summer.

 _____

4 We went to Brazil <u>last summer</u>.

 _____

5 I didn't like the film <u>because the story was boring</u>.

 _____

6 <u>Georgia's</u> poem was the best in the class.

 _____

Pairwork

Work in pairs. Take turns to ask and answer questions using the words from this unit.

Who is your best friend?

When did you meet her?

Teresa.

Five years ago, at school.

Writing

Write a letter to your teacher. Ask six questions.

Present perfect simple: regular and irregular verbs

> I've had a great time with you all.

> It's been fun. Now, smile for the camera!

Present perfect simple: regular verbs

Affirmative	Negative	Question
I have (I've) walked	I have not (haven't) walked	Have I walked?
you have (you've) walked	you have not (haven't) walked	Have you walked?
he has (he's) walked	he has not (hasn't) walked	Has he walked?
she has (she's) walked	she has not (hasn't) walked	Has she walked?
it has (it's) walked	it has not (hasn't) walked	Has it walked?
we have (we've) walked	we have not (haven't) walked	Have we walked?
you have (you've) walked	you have not (haven't) walked	Have you walked?
they have (they've) walked	they have not (haven't) walked	Have they walked?

Short answers

Yes, I have.	No, I haven't.	Yes, it has.	No, it hasn't.
Yes, you have.	No, you haven't.	Yes, we have.	No, we haven't.
Yes, he has.	No, he hasn't.	Yes, you have.	No, you haven't.
Yes, she has.	No, she hasn't.	Yes, they have.	No, they haven't.

We use the present perfect simple to talk about:

* things that happened in the past, when we don't say when they happened. We often use it to talk about experiences. Sometimes we use the word *already*.
  *She **has visited** lots of places in Japan.*
  *I **have already eaten** my lunch.*

* things which finished a short time ago.
  We often use the word *just*.
  *Your parents **have just left**.*
  *He **has just been** to the shops.*

* things that have not finished. We often use the word *yet*.
  *She **hasn't taken** her medicine **yet**.*
  ***Have** we **bought** Grandma a present **yet**?*

The present perfect simple of regular verbs is formed with the auxiliary verb *have/has* and the past participle of the main verb. We form the past participle of regular verbs with the ending *-ed*, as we do for the past simple. The same spelling rules apply (see Unit 13).

We put the word *not* after the word *have/has* to make the negative form.
*Elias **has not made** his bed today.*
*They **haven't written** the postcards.*

We put the word *have/has* before the subject to make the question form.
***Have you brushed** your teeth?*
***Has** Alex **prepared** the food for dinner?*

1 Complete the sentences with the present perfect simple.

1 She __has finished__ (finish) all her work.
2 I _____ (not cook) lunch yet.
3 They _____ (talk) for nearly three hours.
4 She _____ (visit) her cousins a lot this year.
5 You _____ (not tidy) your bedroom today.
6 My parents _____ (travel) all over Europe.
7 We _____ (close) the shop.
8 I _____ (live) here for five years.

2 Complete the questions with the present perfect simple. Then answer the questions.

1 ____Has he arrived____ (he / arrive) at the hotel? ✗
  No, he hasn't.
2 _____ (you / try) to do the exercises? ✔
  _____
3 _____ (they / talk) about the problem? ✗
  _____
4 _____ (she / open) the window? ✗
  _____
5 _____ (the children / stop) playing? ✔
  _____
6 _____ (it / rain) this month? ✗
  _____
7 _____ (the students / study) hard this year? ✔
  _____
8 _____ (Dad / clean) the house? ✔
  _____

Present perfect simple: irregular verbs

The past participle of irregular verbs is not formed with the ending -ed. We form the past participle of these verbs in different ways. (See the irregular verbs list on page 128.)

do → did → done   find → found → found

Notes

The verb go has two past participles: gone and been.

We use have/has gone to say that someone has gone somewhere and has not come back yet. *Miriam* **has gone** to the shop to get some milk.

We use have/has been to say that someone went somewhere and has come back. *He* **has been** to Kenya.

3 **Complete the table.**

Verb	Past simple	Past participle
be	was/were	been
come	came	
do	did	
draw	drew	
drink	drank	
eat	ate	
go	went	
have	had	
make	made	
sit	sat	
speak	spoke	
stand	stood	
take	took	
teach	taught	
write	wrote	

4 **Complete the sentences with the present perfect simple.**

1 I _haven't drunk_ (not drink) all my water yet.

2 We _____ (do) all the exercises.

3 They _____ (not eat) all the chocolates yet.

4 I _____ (lose) my bag!

5 We _____ (already / swim) five kilometres today.

6 I _____ (not buy) any new clothes for a long time.

7 He _____ (sleep) for a long time.

8 We _____ (have) a really wonderful holiday.

5 **Complete the questions with the present perfect simple. Then answer the questions.**

1 _____Has she found_____ (she / find) her keys? ✔

   _Yes, she has._____

2 _____ (they / spend) all their money? ✗

   _____

3 _____ (he / speak) to his teacher? ✔

   _____

4 _____ (she / see) the Sydney Opera House? ✔

   _____

5 _____ (we / meet) his parents before? ✗

   _____

6 _____ (you / learn) all the irregular verbs? ✔

   _____

7 _____ (the lesson / begin)? ✗

   _____

8 _____ (they / buy) enough food? ✔

   _____

6 **Write sentences with *already* and *yet*.**

tidy the cupboards ✗

make the bed ✔

wash the car ✗

do the shopping ✗

clean the kitchen ✔

go for a run ✗

1 I haven't tidied the cupboards yet.

2 _____

3 _____

4 _____

5 _____

6 _____

Think about it!

Look at the position of *already* and *yet* in the sentences.

*I have **already** finished.*

*I haven't finished it **yet**.*

Pairwork

Work in pairs. Take turns to ask and answer the questions below.

* Have you visited any interesting places this year?
* Have you seen any good films this year?
* Have you read any good books this year?
* Have you learnt many new English words this year?
* Have you made any new friends this year?
* Have you been ill this year?
* Have you been to any birthday parties this year?

Writing

Write a short paragraph about your year.
What have you done? What haven't you done?

1 **Complete the table.**

Adjective	Comparative	Superlative
bad	worse	the worst
big		
comfortable		
difficult		
easy		
good		
heavy		
hot		
intelligent		
interesting		
light		
short		
small		
tall		
young		

2 **Complete the sentences with *be going to* and the verb in brackets.**

1 I _____ am going to have _____ (have) a shower.

2 They _____ (not buy) a new flat.

3 We _____ (not eat) at a restaurant this evening.

4 It _____ (be) sunny tomorrow.

5 We _____ (win) the match tomorrow!

6 I _____ (not study) for my exams tonight.

7 He _____ (not wear) his new jeans.

8 She _____ (meet) her friends next week.

3 Complete the questions with *be going to*. Then answer the questions.

1 _____Are you going to walk_____
(you / walk) to the bus stop? ✔
Yes, I am.

2 _____
the piano this afternoon? (she / practise) ✗
_____

3 _____
(they / call) us tomorrow? ✔
_____

4 _____
(he / work) this evening? ✗
_____

5 _____
(it / rain) all day? ✗
_____

6 _____
(I / see) you soon? ✔
_____

7 _____
(we / meet) at the station? ✔
_____

8 _____
(he / win) the race? ✗
_____

4 Complete the sentences with the future simple.

1 I _____will be_____ (be) very happy to see you.
2 She _____ (not be) at the same school next year.
3 We _____ (cook) for you today.
4 They _____ (do) it again.
5 I _____ (not invite) her for dinner.
6 I _____ (open) the door for you!
7 They _____ (bring) the presents with them when they visit us.
8 We _____ (not arrive) late for lunch.

5 Complete the questions with the future simple. Then answer the questions.

1 _____Will you try_____ (you / try) harder at school next year? ✔
Yes, I will.

2 _____ (he / get) back early? ✗
_____

3 _____ (she / feel) better tomorrow? ✔
_____

4 _____ (you / buy) me something from the shop? ✔
_____

5 _____ (they / be) on the bus? ✗
_____

6 _____ (he / have) time to help us? ✗
_____

7 _____ (you / write) soon? ✔
_____

8 _____ (they / be) tired after their trip? ✔
_____

6 **Circle the correct answer.**

1   Who *closed* / *did close* the window?

2   Who *did you write* / *you wrote* to?

3   What *did he see* / *he saw*?

4   What *smells* / *does smell* so nice?

5   Which bike *you like* / *do you like* best?

6   Which jacket *costs* / *does cost* more?

7   Where *he went* / *did he go*?

8   Why *are you* / *you are* sad?

7 **Complete the table.**

Verb	Past simple	Past participle
buy	bought	bought
catch	caught	
draw	drew	
drink	drank	
eat	ate	
go	went	
know	knew	
make	made	
sing	sang	
sit	sat	
speak	spoke	
spend	spent	
swim	swam	
take	took	
think	thought	

8 **Complete the sentences with the correct form of the present perfect simple.**

1   I ___have lost___ (lose) my keys again!

2   You _____ (run) ten kilometres today!

3   I _____ (not buy) any food from the supermarket.

4   We _____ (have) a great time!

5   She _____ (not see) her brother recently.

6   They _____ (write) an email to their cousins.

7   I _____ (do) all my jobs for today!

8   They _____ (swim) in the lake.

9   **Write sentences and questions with the present perfect simple.**

1   you / not clean / your room / yet

    You haven't cleaned your room yet.

2   my parents / visit / a lot of places

    _____

3   we / already finish /our breakfast

    _____

4   I / not live / here / for long

    _____

5   your daughter / always be / good at sports / ?

    _____

6   they / ask / about the holiday / ?

    _____

10   **Complete the questions with the present perfect simple. Then answer the questions.**

1   _____Have you visited_____ (you / visit) Argentina? ✗

    No, I haven't.

2   _____ (she / find) her keys? ✔

    _____

3   _____ (he / buy) a new motorbike? ✗

    _____

4   Where is Amu? _____ (she / go) to her friend's house? ✔

    _____

5   _____ (you / see) that film? ✔

    _____

6   _____ (he / arrive) in Poland? ✗

    _____

7   _____ (you / sell) your house? ✔

    _____

8   _____ (they / talk) about the problem? ✗

    _____

11   **Circle the correct answer.**

1   They didn't *bought* / *buy* any nice clothes.

2   Have you *meet* / *met* his wife?

3   They *haven't* / *didn't* clean the house yesterday.

4   Does he *teach* / *taught* at your school?

5   She *have* / *has* driven for nearly five hours today!

6   She *came* / *come* to the party last night.

7   Have you *flew* / *flown* in a helicopter?

8   I *broke* / *broken* two glasses last week.

1 **Find and write.**

1   My hair isn't curly; it's _____straight_____ .   g h t a i s t r

2   I've got fair hair and _____ eyes.   n e r e g

3   I'm not from a town. I'm from a _____ .   g i v a l l e

4   My _____ is 4 Gate Street.   a s r e s d d

5   I've got five brothers. I've got a big _____ .   l a f i m y

6   I've got three brothers and a _____ .   r i s s e t

7   _____ is my favourite sport.   b t l o l f a o

8   My hobbies are tennis and _____ .   w r i n g a d

2 **Read Judy's description. Answer the questions.**

Hello! My name's Judy. I'm twelve years old. I've got fair hair and blue eyes. I'm from England. I live in a village with my family.

My mum's got brown hair and green eyes. Her name's Anna. My dad's name's Peter. He's got dark hair and blue eyes.

My hobbies are drawing and tennis. I play tennis with my best friend, Carla. It's our favourite sport.

1   How old is Judy?

         _____twelve_____

2   Where's she from?

       _____

3   What colour eyes has she got?

       _____

4   What's her mum's name?

       _____

5   What are her hobbies?

       _____

6   What's her best friend's name?

       _____

3 **Read again. In which paragraph does Judy**

1   talk about her best friend? ___

2   tell us her name?   ___

3   tell us about her family?   ___

4 **Complete Judy's writing plan.**

Paragraph 1: ¹ _____ , say how old I am, say what I look like, say where I'm from, say where I live

Paragraph 2: say who my parents are and ² _____

Paragraph 3: my hobbies, ³ _____ and what we do together

5 **Read another description. Complete the description with the sentences from the box.**

He's got curly hair and dark eyes.
Her name's Elena.
My hobbies are playing the piano and football.
I live in a town with my family.
~~I'm ten years old.~~

Hello! My name's Lucas. ¹ _I'm ten years old._

I've got curly hair and green eyes. I'm from Argentina.

² _____

My sister's got dark hair and brown eyes.

³ _____

My brother's name is Marcos.

⁴ _____

⁵ _____ I play the piano and I play football with my best friend, David. We have a great time.

Now it's your turn!

6 **Use Judy's writing plan to make notes for your description in the plan below.**

My writing plan notes

Paragraph 1: _____

Paragraph 2: _____

Paragraph 3: _____

7 **Now use your writing plan notes to write a description about yourself. Write in your notebook.**

1 **Look and write.**

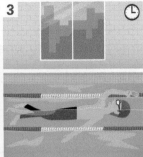

1 r <u>e</u> a d <u>i</u> n g
2 r __ n __ __ __ g
3 s __ __ m __ __ __ g
4 b __ __ k __ __ b __ __ l
5 b __ d __ __ __ t __ n
6 s __ __ p __ i __ g

2 **Read Emilio's description of Hasan's Saturdays. Answer the questions.**

<u>Hasan's Saturdays</u>

Hasan's got lots of free time on Saturdays. Every Saturday, he wakes up early and he has breakfast. After breakfast, he often goes swimming at the sports centre. Then, he goes home and he draws in his bedroom.

At one o'clock, Hasan has lunch. After lunch, he watches TV and then he usually plays football in the park with his friends.

In the evenings, he usually listens to music and then he draws again. Drawing is his favourite hobby. Sometimes, his cousin goes to see him. At night, he always reads before he goes to sleep.

1 When has Hasan got lots of free time?   <u>on Saturdays</u>
2 Where does Hasan go swimming?   _____
3 Who does Hasan play football with?   _____
4 When does Hasan listen to music?   _____
5 How many times does Hasan draw on Saturdays?   _____
6 Who sometimes comes to see Hasan?   _____

3 **Read again. In which paragraph does Emilio say what Hasan does**

1 at night?   ___
2 in the morning?   ___
3 after lunch?   ___

4 **Complete Emilio's writing plan.**

Title: Hasan's Saturdays

Paragraph 1: say when he's got free time, ¹ _____

Paragraph 2: say when he has lunch, ² _____

Paragraph 3: say what he does in the evenings, ³ _____

5 **Read another description. Use the pictures and the words from the box to complete the description.**

★★★★   ★★★   –   ★   ★★

never –
sometimes ★
often ★★
usually ★★★
always ★★★★

Magda's Sundays

Magda's got lots of free time on Sundays. Every Sunday, she wakes up early and she drinks some water. She ¹ _____ never _____ has breakfast. After her drink, she ² _____ rides her bike to the sports centre. Then, she plays basketball with her friends.

At twelve o'clock, Magda has lunch. After lunch, she ³ _____ listens to music in the living room and then she ⁴ _____ paints in her bedroom.

In the evenings, Magda hasn't got a lot of free time. She ⁵ _____ does her homework. At night, she sometimes listens to music before she goes to sleep.

Now it's your turn!

6 **Use Emilio's writing plan, the pictures and the correct adverbs to make notes for your description. The description begins: *Ana has got lots of free time on Sundays!***

Morning   Afternoon   Evening

a  b  c  d  e  f

★★★   ★★★★   ★   ★★   ★★★   –

My writing plan notes

Title: _____

Paragraph 1: _____

Paragraph 2: _____

Paragraph 3: _____

7 **Now use your writing plan notes to write a description of Ana's Sundays. Write in your notebook.**

1 **Find and write.**

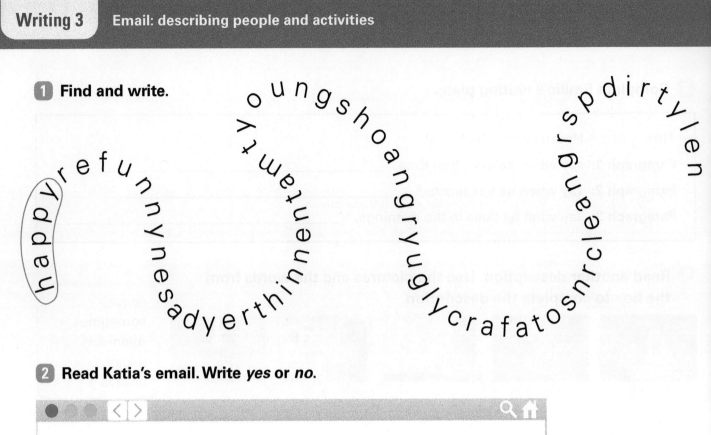

happy refunnynesadyerthinneuntamtyoungshoangryuglycrafatosnrcleaugrspdirtylen

2 **Read Katia's email. Write *yes* or *no*.**

Hi, Ada!

How are you? Thanks for your email. I'm in the garden with Dad and my cousins Maria, Max and Eleni.

My cousins are very nice. Maria's tall and thin. She's eight. Eleni's only three. She's the youngest. Max is the oldest, but he's quite short.

I'm having a great time! Max is happy too. He's playing football with Dad. Eleni's watering the plants with Mum. She's very wet, but she's laughing a lot. Maria is swimming in the pool. She can swim very well, not like me!

What are you doing? Email me soon!

Katia

1 Katia's cousins are in the garden.   _____yes_____
2 Maria is the youngest.   _____
3 Max is older than Maria and Eleni.   _____
4 Max is wet.   _____
5 Dad is playing football with Eleni.   _____
6 Maria can swim better than Katia.   _____

3 **Read again. In which paragraph does Katia**

1 say where she is?   ___
2 say what her cousins are doing? ___
3 describe her cousins?   ___

4 **Complete Katia's writing plan.**

Greeting: Hi!

Paragraph 1: [1] _____ , say who I'm with

Paragraph 2: [2] _____

Paragraph 3: say I'm having a great time, [3] _____

Ending: What are you doing? Email me soon!

Sign off: Katia

5 **Read another email. Complete the email with the sentences from the box.**

Email me soon.
~~Hi, Aran!~~
I'm having a good time!
He's great!
Thanks for your email.

[1] Hi, Aran! _____

How are you? [2] _____ I'm at my friend's house with his sister and brother.

Danny is a new school friend.
[3] _____ Rosa's really funny. She's fourteen, so she's older. Sam's five. He's got curly hair and a round face.

[4] _____ I'm watching a film with Danny. Sam is the kitchen. He's baking a cake with his dad. Rosa is playing a video game. She's really good.

What are you doing? [5] _____

Jay

Now it's your turn!

6 **Use Katia's writing plan to make notes for your email to a friend below.**

My writing plan notes

Greeting: _____

Paragraph 1: _____

Paragraph 2: _____

Paragraph 3: _____

Ending: _____

Sign off: _____

7 **Now use your writing plan notes to write an email to your friend about other people. Write in your notebook.**

1 Look and write.

1 s _t_ _r_ _e_ _e_ t
2 c _ _ _ e _ a
3 f _ _ t
4 s _ _ e _ _ _ _ k _ t
5 h _ _ _ e
6 s _ _ a _ e

2 Read Alex's email. Write *yes* or *no*.

From: Alex   **To:** Stefan   **Subject:** My neighbourhood

Hello Stefan,

How are you? Let me tell you about my neighbourhood. I live in a street in the city centre. I've got good friends here and lots of my friends live near me. It's a great place!

There are fun places to go to in my neighbourhood. There are shops, cafés and there's also a sports centre opposite my house. There's a very big cinema next to the sports centre and there's a swimming pool in the neighbourhood too.

Come and visit me on Saturday! We can go shopping, swim in the pool or play basketball at the sports centre. I live between the bank and the Cool Café at 36 Hope Street. You can come on the number 4 bus. It stops at the bus stop in front of the library.

Let me know!

Alex

1   Alex lives in the city centre.   _____yes_____
2   Lots of Alex's friends live in his neighbourhood.   _____
3   Alex lives in a bad neighbourhood.   _____
4   There's a sports centre next to Alex's house.   _____
5   Alex and Stefan can go swimming at the sports centre.   _____
6   There's a bus stop in front of the library.   _____

3 Read again. In which paragraph does Alex

1   say how to get to his house?   ___
2   talk about the people in his neighbourhood?   ___
3   describe his neighbourhood?   ___

4 Complete Alex's writing plan.

> **Greeting:** Hello!
>
> **Paragraph 1:** say where I live, ¹ _____ , say it's a great place
>
> **Paragraph 2:** ² _____
>
> **Paragraph 3:** ask Stefan to come, say what we can do together, ³ _____
>
> **Ending:** Let me know!
>
> **Sign off:** Alex

5 Read another email and look at
the map. Complete the email
with the words from the box.

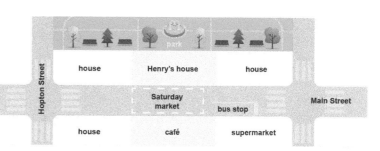

behind	between	~~in~~
in front of	next to	opposite

Hello Omar,

Let me tell you about my neighbourhood. I live ¹ _____in_____ a house in a village.

There aren't many places in the village. There's a café ² _____ my house and there's
a supermarket ³ _____ the café. On Saturdays, there's a market ⁴ _____ my
house and the café. There's also a park ⁵ _____ my house.

Come and visit me on Saturday. Catch the number 16 bus. It stops at the bus stop
⁶ _____ the supermarket.

Let me know!

Henry

Now it's your turn!

6 Use Alex's writing plan to make notes for your email about your neighbourhood below.

> **My writing plan notes**
>
> **Greeting:** _____
>
> **Paragraph 1:** _____
>
> **Paragraph 2:** _____
>
> **Paragraph 3:** _____
>
> **Ending:** _____
>
> **Sign Off:** _____

7 Now use your writing plan notes to write an email about your neighbourhood.
Write in your notebook.

1 **Find and complete the words.**

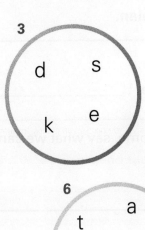

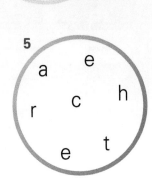

1   g eography
2   h_____
3   d_____
4   l_____
5   t_____
6   m_____

2 **Read Suma's diary entry. Answer the questions.**

Friday 12ᵗʰ December

I had a nice day today. In the morning, Lucy came and we rode our bikes to school. I took my new school bag. It's great!

Our first lesson was history. We had a test, but it went well. Then, we had maths. I like maths, but Lucy thinks it's difficult. She didn't understand, so Ms Deeb helped her. She's a really good teacher.

I ate pasta for lunch and then I played football in the playground. Lucy's brother came to play with us. He plays football for the school. After lunch, we had a geography lesson and then we did some drawing. I was very pleased with my picture.

In the evening, Lucy came to my house. We didn't do our homework – we watched TV. It's Friday night!

Good night!

1   What did Suma take to school?

    _____ her new bag _____

2   Who is Ms Deeb?

    _____

3   Where did Suma play football?

    _____

4   Who came to play a game of football?

    _____

5   What was Suma pleased with?

    _____

6   What did the children do in the evening?

    _____

3 **Read again. In which paragraph does Suma talk about**

1   lunch?   3
2   her first lesson?   ___
3   homework?   ___
4   what she took to school?   ___

116

4 **Complete Suma's writing plan.**

Paragraph 1: say yesterday was nice, say who came, say how we went to school,
¹ _____say what I took to school_____

Paragraph 2: ² _____ , my second lesson

Paragraph 3: ³ _____ , say what I did after I ate, my
afternoon lessons

Paragraph 4: say who came in the evening, ⁴ _____ ,
say what we didn't do

5 **Read another diary entry. Complete the diary entry with the phrases from the box.**

~~in the morning~~
in the evening
our first
then
after lunch

Thursday 3ʳᵈ March

I had a boring day today! ¹ _____In the morning_____ ,
I walked to school with my friend Tim. I took my English project in.

² _____ lesson was English with
Mr Smith. ³ _____ , we had history.
I don't like English or history, but Tim likes them. He thinks they're fun!

I ate a sandwich for lunch and then I read a book in the classroom.
Mr Smith was there and he talked to me about the book.
⁴ _____ , we had a maths lesson
and then we played tennis. I don't like tennis!

⁵ _____ , Tim and Deepak came to
my house. We did our homework together. It was good to finish it, but it was
a bit boring! We didn't have time to play video games. ☹

Now it's your turn!

6 **Use Suma's writing plan to make notes for your diary entry about school below.**

My writing plan notes
Paragraph 1: _____
Paragraph 2: _____
Paragraph 3: _____
Paragraph 4: _____

7 **Now use your writing plan notes to write a diary entry about a day at your school.
Write in your notebook.**

1 **Look and write.**

1 c _h_ _e_ _e_ _s_ _e_
2 b __ n __ n __ __ __
3 c __ __ e
4 e __ g __
5 g __ a __ __ __ __
6 m __ l __
7 c __ __ __ p __
8 b __ __ a __

2 **Read Lena's review. Write *yes* or *no*.**

Lunch at Joe's Café by Lena

Last Saturday, I had lunch at Joe's Café. It's near the library in the city centre. I went with my best friend, Dani.

First, we got some drinks because we were very thirsty. There wasn't any juice, but there were these amazing milkshakes. I had a strawberry milkshake. It was delicious! Then, we asked for some food. I had some tasty noodles with vegetables, and Dani had a pizza. I love noodles. Dani liked the pizza, but it was too big. I tried some pizza and it was good.

I think Joe's Café is a nice place to eat. The food is tasty and the people are very friendly. You can also eat outside. The best thing is, it isn't expensive. I'd like to go again.

1 Lena and Dani went to Joe's Café on Saturday. _____ yes _____
2 There weren't any milkshakes. _____
3 Lena had noodles. _____
4 Dani's pizza was too small. _____
5 It was expensive. _____
6 Lena didn't like Joe's Café. _____

3 **Read again. In which paragraph does Lena say**

1 she'd like to go to Joe's Café again? ___
2 who she went with? ___
3 what food they had? ___

4 **Complete Lena's writing plan.**

Title: Lunch at Joe's Café

Paragraph 1: say when and where I went, ¹ _____

Paragraph 2: drinks, ² _____ , say what food we
              liked/didn't like

Paragraph 3: say what I liked/didn't like about Joe's Café,
              ³ _____

5 **Read another review. Circle the correct words.**

Dinner at The Oasis Café

Last Wednesday, I had dinner at The Oasis Café. It's next to
the cinema in George Street. I went with my brother Erik.

First, we got ¹ *some* / *any* drinks because we were hot.
We wanted some apple juice but there ² *wasn't / weren't*
any. I had ³ *a / some* glass of milk and Erik had a ⁴ *bottle /
bottles* of cola. Then, we asked for some food. I had a cheese
sandwich and ⁵ *some / any* crisps. Erik had ⁶ *a / an* cheese
burger and chips. He liked the burger, but he didn't like the
chips because they were cold. He also had cake, but it was
too sweet. I didn't have cake – I had some fruit. It was OK.

I don't think The Oasis Café is the best place to eat.
The food ⁷ *isn't / aren't* great, and the people ⁸ *isn't / aren't*
very friendly. Also, it's very expensive. I wouldn't like to
go again.

Now it's your turn!

6 **Use Lena's writing plan to make notes for your review of a café below.**

My writing plan notes

Title: _____

Paragraph 1: _____

Paragraph 2: _____

Paragraph 3: _____

7 **Now use your writing plan notes to write a review of the café. Write in your notebook.**

1 **Match 1–5 with a–e.**

1 put on   e
2 take off ___
3 wash   ___
4 wear   ___
5 clean   ___

2 **Read Taro's note. Answer the questions.**

Hi Mum!

I'm with Sam. We're going shopping for our weekend away in London. You know – we're going to stay with his uncle. I need a new scarf, so I'm going to buy one at the shopping centre.

I want to take my black jeans and my blue T-shirt to London, but my T-shirt is dirty. Can you wash it for me, please? 😊 Also, I can't find my black boots. Do you know where they are? I wore them the other day. I remember taking them off, but I can't remember where I put them. I'd like to clean them.

Don't worry about making me any food tonight – I'm not going to come home for dinner. I'm going to eat pasta at Sam's house.

Thanks, Mum!

Taro

1   Who's Taro with?   _____Sam_____
2   Who are they going to stay with at the weekend?   _____
3   What's Taro going to buy?   _____
4   What is dirty?   _____
5   What does Taro want his mum to find?   _____
6   Where's Taro going to have dinner?   _____

3 **Read again. In which paragraph does Taro say**

1   what clothes he's going to take to London?   ___
2   where he and Sam are going for dinner?   ___
3   who he's with?   ___

4 **Complete Taro's writing plan.**

Greeting: Hi!

Paragraph 1: ¹ _____ , say what we're going to do

Paragraph 2: ² _____ , things to wash/find/clean

Paragraph 3: ³ _____

Ending: Thanks!

Sign off: Taro

5 **Read another note. Divide it into paragraphs.**

Hi Dad!

I'm with Ada. We're going shopping for our weekend in Italy. You know – we're going to stay with Ada's grandma. I want a new jacket and I'm going to buy one at the market. I want to take my black trousers and T-shirt to Italy, but my trousers are dirty. Can you wash them for me, please? 😊 Also, do you know where my green suitcase is? I want to clean it before I go. I had it last summer, but I can't remember where I put it! I'm going to come home for dinner at 7:00. Please can we have a pizza? You don't need to make dinner for Ada – she's going to eat at her house.

Thanks, Dad!

Sara

Now it's your turn!

6 **Use Taro's writing plan to make notes for your note below.**

My writing plan notes

Greeting: _____

Paragraph 1: _____

Paragraph 2: _____

Paragraph 3: _____

Ending: _____

Sign off: _____

7 **Now use your writing plan notes to write a note to your mum or dad. Write in your notebook.**

1 **Find and complete the words.**

1   k c e a

2   i s m c u

3   p a t y r

4   p e r s e t n

5   e m g a s

6   e d n a c

1   c <u>ake</u>

2   m_____

3   p_____

4   p_____

5   g_____

6   d_____

2 **Read Billy's invitation. Answer the questions.**

Dear _____<u>Hans</u>_____ ,

I'll be eleven on Friday! Please come to my party.
It's at my house on Saturday at seven o'clock.
It'll be fantastic!

There'll be juice and lots of tasty food. We'll have
burgers, chips and ice cream, and a big birthday
cake too. Later, we'll play some games with Mr
Fun and then we'll dance to some great music.

Call me! My phone number is 01779 254877
and my address is 2 King's Road.

See you there!

Billy

1   When will Billy have his party?
    <u>on Saturday</u>

2   Where will Billy have his party?
    _____

3   What will the children drink?
    _____

4   Who will the children play games with?
    _____

5   What will the children do after they play?
    _____

6   Where does Billy live?
    _____

3 **Read again. In which paragraph does Billy say**

1   what they'll do at the party?   ___

2   what time the party is?   ___

3   what his address is?   ___

4 **Complete Billy's writing plan.**

> **Greeting:** Dear ...
>
> **Paragraph 1:** say how old I'll be, ask my friend to come, say where the party is,
> 1 _____
>
> **Paragraph 2:** say what we will drink and eat, 2 _____
>
> **Paragraph 3:** give my phone number, 3 _____
>
> **Ending:** See you there!
>
> **Sign off:** Billy

5 **Read another invitation. Complete the invitation with the phrases from the box.**

> It's at my house   My phone number is
> ~~Please come to~~   See you
> There'll be lots of

Dear Kamala,

I'll be twelve at the weekend! 1 _____ Please come to _____ my party.

2 _____ on Saturday at six o'clock. It'll be fun!

3 _____ juice, pizzas and sandwiches to eat, and we'll have birthday cake too. Later, we'll swim in the pool.

Call me! 4 _____ 01333 546378 and my address is 5 Hatton Street.

5 _____ there!

May

Now it's your turn!

6 **Use Billy's writing plan to make notes for your letter of invitation below.**

> **My writing plan notes**
>
> **Greeting:** _____
>
> **Paragraph 1:** _____
>
> **Paragraph 2:** _____
>
> **Paragraph 3:** _____
>
> **Ending:** _____
>
> **Sign off:** _____

7 **Now use your writing plan notes to write a letter of invitation to your birthday party. Write in your notebook.**

1 Find and complete the words.

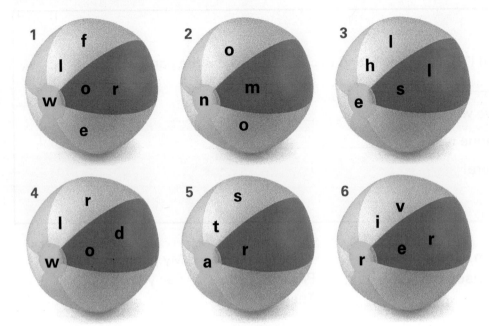

1   f _lower_ _____
2   m_____
3   s_____
4   w_____
5   s_____
6   r_____

2 Read Marco's postcard. Answer the questions.

Hi Tom!

I'm on holiday at my friend's house in the mountains. The place where we're staying is very nice, but it's very quiet. I can't sleep at night because there aren't any noisy cars or buses!

We're having a great time! Every day, we go for a walk in a forest near a river. There are lots of animals and plants there. We walk near the river, but we don't go swimming. The water is very cold! We usually take some bread and cheese with us for lunch. In the evenings, we eat at home or we ride our bikes to a village where there's a café. We usually eat chicken and vegetables or burgers and salad. Yummy!

At the moment, I'm writing my postcards here in my bedroom. I'm going to go to bed soon because I'm tired.

See you soon!

Marco

30

Tom Wong

42 Hall Street

Hebdon

1   Who is Marco on holiday with?
    _____ his friend _____

2   What can't Marco do at night?
    _____

3   What is near the river?
    _____

4   Why doesn't Marco go swimming?
    _____

5   When does Marco go to the village?
    _____

6   Why is Marco going to go to bed?
    _____

3 Read again. In which paragraph does Marco talk about

1   what he's doing now?   ___
2   where he's staying?   ___
3   what he does in the evenings? ___

4 **Complete Marco's writing plan.**

> Greeting: Hi!
> **Paragraph 1:** say who I'm with, ¹ _____ , say what the place is like
> **Paragraph 2:** say what we do in the mornings, say what we have for lunch,
>   ² _____
> **Paragraph 3:** ³ _____ , say what I'm going to do soon
> **Ending:**   See you soon!
> **Sign off:** Marco

5 **Read another postcard. Complete the**
   postcard with the words from the box.

> and (x2)   because (x2)   ~~but~~   or

> Hi Dasha!
>
> I'm on holiday with my best friend in Italy. The village where we're staying is very beautiful,
> ¹ ___but___ it's very small. We can't go shopping ² _____ there aren't
> any shops, but there's a fantastic market every weekend.
>
> We're having a great time! Every day, we wake up early and we go for a walk on a beach
> near our house. There are lots of shells ³ _____ rocks there. We go fishing
> ⁴ _____ we also go swimming every day. We usually take sandwiches with us
> for lunch. In the evenings, we eat at the restaurant in the village ⁵ _____ we
> cook at home. We often cook fish from the river with vegetables from the garden. Yummy!
>
> At the moment, I'm writing my postcards outside. I'm watching the moon and the stars.
> I'm going to go to bed soon ⁶ _____ it's late.
>
> See you soon!
>
> Viri

Now it's your turn!

6 **Use Marco's writing plan to make notes for your postcard to a friend below.**

> **My writing plan notes**
> **Greeting:**   _____
> **Paragraph 1:** _____
> **Paragraph 2:** _____
> **Paragraph 3:** _____
> **Ending:**   _____
> **Sign off:**   _____

7 **Now use your writing plan notes to write a postcard to a friend about your holiday.**
   Write in your notebook.

125

1 Complete the crossword.

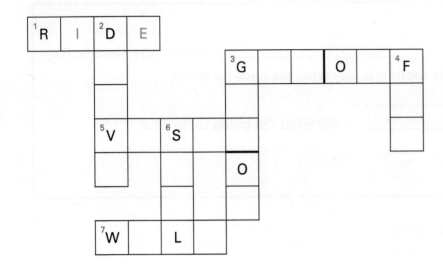

Across   Down

¹R I ²D E

³G O ⁴F

⁵V ⁶S

O

⁷W L

2 Read Cara's essay. Write _yes_ or _no_.

Travelling by train

Many people travel by train every day, to go to work, to go on holiday or to visit friends and family. But is travelling by train fun?

There are good things about travelling by train. It's exciting and you travel fast. You can also look out of the window and see towns, cities and the countryside as you're travelling. I like to read a book, and sometimes you can buy a drink or a snack on board. Last week, I went to the beach by train. It was great!

There are some bad things about travelling by train too. The tickets are often expensive. Also, sometimes there are problems and there are big delays. Waiting at the train station for a late train is so boring! Finally, the trains often get very busy and you can't sit down.

But I think travelling by train is fun. It's better than flying because you don't have to wait at an airport. I'm going to travel by train when I go on holiday next year.

1   Cara thinks travelling by train is exciting.   _____yes_____

2   You can't look out of the window on trains.   _____

3   Tickets for trains are always cheap.   _____

4   Cara doesn't like waiting for delayed trains.   _____

5   Everyone can sit down on a train.   _____

6   Cara doesn't want travel by train again.   _____

3 Read again. In which paragraph does Cara

1   say why she thinks trains are better than other kinds of transport?   _4_

2   give an example of a bad thing about trains?   ___

3   say what the good things about trains are?   ___

4   say what the essay is going to talk about?   ___

4 **Complete Cara's writing plan.**

Title: Travelling by train

Paragraph 1: ¹ _____ say what the essay is about _____

Paragraph 2: ² _____ , give examples of the good things
about travelling by train

Paragraph 3: say there are bad things about travelling by train,
³ _____

Paragraph 4: ⁴ _____ , say how I'm going to travel next year

5 **Read another essay. Divide it into paragraphs.**

Travelling by ship

Many people travel by ship every day, but is travelling by ship fun? There are lots of good things about travelling by ship. Ships are very big and beautiful. You can watch fish or birds and you can meet people too. Last year, I sailed to France on a big ship. It was great! There are some bad things about travelling by ship too. The tickets aren't very cheap. Also, some people feel ill when they sail. They feel worse when the weather is bad! My dad sailed on a ship last week in the wind and rain. He felt very ill. I think travelling by ship is better than travelling by other kinds of transport. You can meet people and you can sometimes go swimming in a swimming pool on the ship! I'm going to sail to an island when I go on holiday next year.

Now it's your turn!

6 **Use Cara's writing plan to make notes for your essay about a different kind of transport below.**

My writing plan notes

Title: _____

Paragraph 1: _____

Paragraph 2: _____

Paragraph 3: _____

Paragraph 4: _____

7 **Now use your writing plan notes to write an essay about the kind of transport you chose. Write in your notebook.**

Irregular verbs

Infinitive	Past simple	Past participle	Infinitive	Past simple	Past participle
be	was/were	been	lead	led	led
become	became	become	learn	learnt	learnt
begin	began	begun	leave	left	left
blow	blew	blown	lend	lent	lent
break	broke	broken	lose	lost	lost
bring	brought	brought	make	made	made
build	built	built	meet	met	met
buy	bought	bought	pay	paid	paid
catch	caught	caught	put	put	put
choose	chose	chosen	read	read	read
come	came	come	ride	rode	ridden
cut	cut	cut	ring	rang	rung
do	did	done	run	ran	run
draw	drew	drawn	say	said	said
drink	drank	drunk	see	saw	seen
drive	drove	driven	sell	sold	sold
eat	ate	eaten	shine	shone	shone
fall	fell	fallen	sing	sang	sung
feed	fed	fed	sit	sat	sat
feel	felt	felt	sleep	slept	slept
find	found	found	speak	spoke	spoken
fly	flew	flown	spend	spent	spent
forget	forgot	forgotten	stand	stood	stood
get	got	got	swim	swam	swum
give	gave	given	take	took	taken
go	went	gone	teach	taught	taught
grow	grew	grown	tell	told	told
have	had	had	think	thought	thought
hear	heard	heard	understand	understood	understood
hit	hit	hit	wake	woke	woken
hurt	hurt	hurt	wear	wore	worn
keep	kept	kept	win	won	won
know	knew	known	write	wrote	written